CONTEMPORARY
AFRICAN POLITICS

A Comparative Study of Political Transition
to Democratic Legitimacy

Edited by

Bamidele A. Ojo

University Press of America,® Inc.
Lanham • New York • Oxford

Copyright © 1999 by
University Press of America,® Inc.
4720 Boston Way
Lanham, Maryland 20706

12 Hid's Copse Rd.
Cumnor Hill, Oxford OX2 9JJ

Library of Congress Cataloging-in-Publication Data

Contemporary African politics : a comparative study of political
transition to democratic legitimacy / edited by Bamidele A. Ojo.
p.   cm.
Includes bibliographical references.
1. Democracy—Africa. 2. Democratization—Africa. I. Ojo,
Bamidele A.
JQ1879.A15C675   1999   320.96'09'049—dc21   98-32387 CIP

ISBN 0-7618-1327-6 (cloth: alk. ppr.)
ISBN 0-7618-1328-4 (pbk: alk. ppr.)

Contents

Preface   Contemporary African Politics   v
           In   A   New World Order

PART I   Democracy and Democratization.   1

Chapter 1   The Democracy Discourse in   1
           International Relations:
           Identity, Development and Africa.
           Kevin Dunn

Chapter 2   International Efforts At   24
           Democracy and Sub-Saharan
           Africa Development.
           Adegboyega A. Somide

Chapter 3   The Military and the   51
             Democratization Process In
             Africa.
             Bamidele A. Ojo

Chapter 4   Africa, Economic Recovery and   64
             Political   Transition.
             Julius Ihonvbere

PART II   Political Transition in   87
             Comparative Perspective.

Chapter 5   Democratic Representation : A   88
             Ugandan Model
             Thomas O'Hara

Chapter 6   Namibia -Africa's Last Colony: 109
             A Democratic Experiment.
             Bamidele A. Ojo

Chapter 7   The Transition To Democracy   125
             In Nigeria :Engaging New
             Possibilities In A Changing
             World Order.
             Austin Ogunsuyi.

Chapter 8   South Africa And Post   154
             Apartheid Democracy.
             Bamidele A. Ojo

Index   161

About the Editor   163

About the Contributors   164

Preface

Contemporary African Politics In a
New World Order

Three decades since independence and there is nothing but political
chaos and economic and social decay which makes one wonder when
and how are the countries of Africa are going to be able to take the
necessary steps towards socio-political and economic development.
Following independence there was tremendous hope for Africa and the
future seemed to indicate tremendous growth and competitive
economies for many African States. But experience has since shown
us the opposite. There has been political and economic stagnation and
indebtedness which engulfed the entire African continent and
therefore obscure the hopes of earlier euphoria.

For the past three decades , we have also witnessed an explosion of
concepts and sometimes contradictory and rather predictive
perspectives on the state of the continent. Moreover and since the end
of the cold war, the focus has been on democratization and democracy
on the continent and the discourse which followed exhibits the same
pattern, in form, in development and in analysis. In an attempt to
impact the contemporary discourse, a panel was organized at the 1997
NorthEast Political Science Association that was held in Philadelphia,
Pennsylvania on the 14th of November, 1997. The Panel on Democracy
and Political Transition In Africa allowed for a diverse analysis of
contemporary African Politics which in essence turned out to be an
interesting and thought provoking exercise and putting all these
excellent debates together in this volume has been as enlightening as
it can ever get.

The focus of the first chapter by Kevin Dunn, on International democratization discourse, argues that the current debates has been created by western hegemonic powers to reflect the needs and interests of these powers because its conceptual framework allows some modes of thoughts while denying others. Kevin also argues that this discourse is closely tied to western discourse of development and the production and practice of these discourse are inextricably linked to representations of Africa and Africans within the international community.

The essence of chapter 2 is the contradictory objective of the various international and local actors attempting to promote political and economic liberalization in sub-Saharan Africa since 1980. In this chapter, Adegboyega Somide argues that the external divergence between international actors and Africans, constitute a major obstacle to any successful transition to market-led economies and democracy. In a non afro-pessimistic tradition, Julius in chapter 3 critique the current superstructural and superficial responses to African predicaments while Bamidele follows up with an examination of the military involvement in the democratization process on the continent. Taking cognizance of the importance of the military as a repository of authorized use of violence, he argues that the disruptive role of the military, as it develops, promotes and sustains its interest within the society, by reconstituting itself as the alternative political force undermines the democratization process in many countries in Africa.

The second part which is focused on the comparative analysis of political transition, begins with Thomas O'Hara's piece on Democratic Representation :A Ugandan Model, presents a case study of one of the unique African experiment at defining and developing a non-party electoral process based on Ugandan domestic characteristics. In chapter 6, Bamidele presents the Namibia's democratic experiment taking cognizance of the role of the United Nations and the dramatic transition made by the South West African People's Organization (SWAPO) from a national liberation organization to a viable political party in a democratic Namibia.

At independence Nigeria exhibited tremendous potential for democratic success and economic development in Africa and today it remains a country totally at an impasse and in Ogunsuyi's piece, he examines the electoral uncertainties in Nigeria and the transition program of the Abacha government and the book ends with Bamidele's synopsis on the post-apartheid democracy in South Africa, wherein the state and the society continues to exhibits the tremendous destabilizing effects of the four decades of the apartheid regime.

PART I: Democracy and Democratization

Chapter 1

The Democracy Discourse In International Relations : Identity, Development And Africa

Kevin Dunn

INTRODUCTION[1]*

The "Third Wave" of democratization is still ebbing and flowing.[2] The recent unrest in Kenya is evidence that there are continuing domestic pressures to democratize African states. While democratic forces remain active throughout the African continent, scholars continue to spill ink debating the promises and pitfalls of African democratic transitions.[3] It is commonplace to note the many stumbles and failures along the path to democracy; for every South Africa, there is a Zambia. This essay seeks to open new ground for discussing democracy in Africa by focusing on the international "democratization discourse."

The arguments in this essay are offered as entry points for future research and theoretical scholarship. My arguments operate at three related levels. First, I argue there currently exists a "democratization discourse" that has been created by Western hegemonic powers to reflect the needs and interests of those powers. Discourses are "the conceptual frameworks which allow some modes of thought and deny others."[4] They exist within a set of specific texts that define and delineate the "reality" of any subject, in this case "democracy."

Importantly, a discourse is not just a set of written or spoken texts, but also "the social practices to which those texts are inextricably linked."[5] The current "democratization discourse" strictly defines what "democracy" can mean and shapes the path "democratization" can follow. Most importantly, the discourse legitimizes certain actions and beliefs while delegitimizing others. It is my contention that this discourse is produced and employed largely outside of the African context, yet has major implications for the events within the continent. The "democratization discourse" is employed by international lending agencies and Western states to define and encourage the transition of African polities to "legitimate" democracies.

The essay's second argument is that this "democratization discourse" is closely tied to the Western discourse on development. In the development discourse, development is conceived solely within the global capitalist economic orthodoxy. What has occurred in the post-Cold War era is the subjugation of the "democratization discourse" to the Western discourse on "development."

The result is that Western forces and international lending agencies -- the International Monetary Fund [IMF] and the World Bank -- are less concerned with "democratizing" African societies as they are in transforming them into open market economies. Market "reform" has been given priority over democracy. The third argument here is that the production and practice of these discourses are inextricably linked to representations of Africa and Africans within the international community.

The representation of African identities constructs a "knowable" subject upon which certain actions can be taken and alternative courses marginalized. For example, constructing Africans as childlike during the colonial era made paternalistic policies legitimate.[6] To understand how these discourses operate, as well as how to challenge these discourses, one must begin with an examination of how and why certain identities are constructed.

Identity And Representation In International Relations

African states do not exist within a vacuum. Rather, they exist within an international society that is comprised of other states and non-state actors. The international society is defined by its common rules, values and institutions. In the current international society, the glue that holds the system together is the Westphalian concept of state sovereignty, territorial integrity and the principle of non-intervention.[7] Within the international society, states recognize the common interest of maintaining these social arrangements. Therefore, the international society is in part self-regulating.[8]

The Westphalian state system was imported to Africa by way of European colonization. Whether or not the resulting nation-state is the "black man's burden"[9] seems immaterial at this point. For good or ill, the nation-state is likely here to stay. Yet, all states are not the same. To claim so would be to ignore the historical process of state construction and evolution. African states were incorporated into the global capitalist system as specialized producers within a global division of labor constructed according to the European powers' needs.[10] Without getting bogged down in the dependency/modernization debate, I assert that African's position in the global division of labor has not changed radically since independence, reflecting the hierarchical structure of the international system.

The international society is a hierarchically ordered system, based on Western hegemony. As Robert Cox has observed, "the hegemonic concept of world order is founded not only upon the regulation of inter-state conflicts but also upon a globally-conceived civil society."[11] Global hegemony is embedded in the combination of social, political and economic structures, and is expressed through universal norms, institutions and mechanisms, particularly international institutions. According to Cox, "(1) [international institutions] embody the rules which facilitate expansion of hegemonic world orders; (2) they are themselves the product of the hegemonic world order; (3) they ideologically legitimate the norms of the world order; (4) they co-opt the elites from peripheral countries and (5) they absorb counter-hegemonic ideas."[12] As I will argue in this essay, hegemonic conceptions of democracy -- "democratization discourses" -- are produced and exercised primarily through hegemonic institutions such as the IMF and World Bank.

By recognizing the modern state society's historical evolution, one can also note how the system becomes self-regulating and self-perpetuating, ensuring continued hegemonic rule and hierarchical divisions.[13] Scholars such as Jackson and Rosberg have observed that the international society perpetuates and regulates itself through the conferring of juridical statehood.[14] Even though a political system may possess some or all of the empirical qualifications of statehood, without certain juridical attributes (i.e. territory and independence) the system is not a state. Juridical attributes of statehood can only be conferred by the international community. Many of Africa's states are therefore juridical, not empirical, entities. The international society allows many of Africa's weak states to persist through juridical recognition, thus sustaining and perpetuating inept and corrupt governments.[15]

While they never use the term directly, Jackson and Rosberg's work illustrates the way "discourse" (in this case, juridical recognition) produces statehood. They also allude to but never address the concept of "identity" in the international community. Jackson and Rosberg realize that the identity of actors is largely determined by their environment. An international actor is not a "state" until the international society recognizes it as one. Shared identities of the self are what distinguish an international society from an international system. As Barry Buzan writes, an international society exists "when units not only recognize each other as being the same type of entity but also are prepared to accord each other equal legal status on that basis."[16]

There is a growing realization within the academic community of the importance of identity[17] in both the practice and theorizing of international relations.[18]   As Buzan observes, "Societies are fundamentally about identity," and the international society is no exception".[19]

The representations of a state's identity influences how it is perceived and treated by others. In the international society, the identities of states affect how they give meaning to themselves and their environment.[20] Identity also helps define the parameters of action available to a state. Roxanne Lynn Doty has pointed out that the representation of Filipinos helped shape the United States' Philippine counterinsurgency policy in the 1950s.[21]

In The Conquest of America, Tzvetan Todorov illustrates how the image of Amerindian identity created by Spanish conquistadors allowed, if not caused, the violent conquest and destruction of the former by the latter.[22] Furthermore, an actor's identity helps shape the hierarchy of social positions of power. In the case of Africa, this hierarchical social positioning is closely linked with its role in the global division of labor and the legacy of colonization.[23]

With regards to Africa, the identities of African states have been produced through representational practices, or, what Roxanne Lynn Doty refers to as "imperial encounters."[24]   Doty argues that the historical encounters between the North and South resulted in the practice of representation of the latter by the former which discursively produced regimes of "truth" and "knowledge".   It is within these discursive representations that identities -- of the African Other and of the European Self -- are produced and contested. For Doty, the representation of the South by the North is also linked to the hegemonic dimensions of global politics. These rhetorical acts establish a relationship of subject

(Europe) and object (Africa). Therefore, these rhetorical acts create a system of hegemonic dominance and justify exploitative acts. As Doty observes, " encounters between the North and the South were (and are) such that the North's representations of 'reality' enabled practices of domination, exploitation, and brutality, practices that probably would have been considered unthinkable, reprehensible, and unjustifiable were an alternative 'reality' taken seriously."[25]

In asymmetric power relationships -- such as those that exist between Africa and the West -- the stronger power has greater authorship of identities and the discourses of "reality." This argument does not imply that the lesser powers (here, Africans) are without agency. Rather, it recognizes the hierarchies in international relations and their implications for the power of African agency. Such an argument helps avoid naive interpretations or pronouncements concerning North-South relations and the unqualified promise of democratization.

In the case of African states, their identities have been largely (though not solely) the result of European colonization, their incorporation into the Western state system, and their continuing role in the global economic order. African states' identities, as well as the identities of Western societies, are closely tied to these discursive representational practices. In the post-Cold War era, the discourse of democratization has gained significance in international relations. It is to this discourse that I now turn.

Democratization Discourses

There is never one single discourse. Rather, at any given time there are numerous discourses contending for primacy. I argue that in the post-Cold War era the rise of a primary "democratization discourse" has marginalized other, alternative discourses on democracy. This dominant discourse is based on narrow, Western conceptions of democracy that are firmly lodged in Western historical experiences and entrenched within the liberal economic tradition. This discourse has been able to marginalize other discourses on democracy because of the continuation of Western hegemony in the international society, as practiced through international lending agencies, and the asymmetric power relationship that exists between Western and African states.

According to the democratization discourse, the African state must meet certain requirements in order to be considered a functioning democracy. This conception of democracy is based on the experiences of Western states.[26] Moreover, representations of Western identities are embedded in this conception of democracy. Western societies define themselves according to such democratic principles. During the Cold War, for example, the First World states were defined as "developed capitalist democracies." The Second and Third Worlds were then defined only through their lack of these characteristics. Such identity classification continues in the post-Cold War era.

For instance, in their text on International Politics, Donald Snow and Eugene Brown divide the world into "tiers". The so-called First Tier is made up of market democracies. The second tier is made up of all others, hierarchically ordered according to their development evolution.[27] The construction and representation of a state's identity in the Westphalian state system has been largely shaped by Western conceptions of democracy, which have become inextricably linked to the "free market" economic system.

In the Cold War and post-Cold War eras, identities within the international system were constructed through exclusionary (hierarchical) acts: democratic/undemocratic, developed/ undeveloped, First World/Third World, rich/poor, North/South, Self/Other. In order for a state to become a legitimate "democracy" requires the adoption of Western democratic standards. Yet, here in lies a paradox that African societies face. Becoming a democracy -- as defined by the democratization discourse -- entails a denial of the Self.

As noted above, the African identity, as represented in the discourses of international politics, is distinctly undemocratic -- on Western terms. To be "democratic" therefore requires a transformation of the African society and identity. This is democratization through self-denial. Much of the pessimism about Africa's ability to "democracy" is actually pessimism about Africa becoming more "Western."

In their 1994 report, the democracy-monitoring Freedom House stated: "While in 1994 the trend toward the extension of formal democracies in [Africa] was unmistakable, the durability of these transitions was far from assured. In part, because of the weakness of independent organized life, of free trade unions, civic organizations, and the private sector."[28] The basis for pessimism is because African societies lack the Western attributes that the dominant "democratization discourse" define as necessary components for "legitimate" democracies. This point is reflected in the writings of Carol Lancaster, who notes that:

> It is important to be realistic about the nature of Africa's new democracies
> or partially liberalized regimes. Even in those countries where political
> liberalization has been the most extensive -- for example, Benin or Zambia
> -- the new regimes are still very different from Western- style democracies.
> First of all, the newly established political institutions are weak and their rules
> of operation are not fully elaborated... Second, the nature of political
> competition in Africa is much different from political competition in
> Western democracies and is likely to remain so for some time.[29]

The path of "legitimate" democratic transformation is laid out in the "democratization discourse" Because this discourse has been produced within a Western context, the path of democratization is reflective of Western states' experiences and ignores African experiences or practices.[30] More importantly, this discourse reflects the interests of Western forces. Herein lies the second paradox facing African societies: the "democratization discourse" is more concerned with the pretense of democracy -- or democratic "window-dressing" -- than the realization and practice of pluralistic politics in Africa. This preoccupation with the facade of democracy is due to the convergence in the post-Cold War era of the Western "democratization discourse" and the Western "development discourse." Or, more correctly, the privileging of development over democracy.

Democracy And Development

Numerous authors have noted the existence and implications of Western-defined " development discourses". In his 1994 study of Lesotho, James Ferguson shows how development institutions generate their own discourses that create a structure of knowledge about the subject, a structure upon which subsequent courses of action are based and alternative courses marginalized.[31] Like democratization discourses, development discourses define and delineate the concept of " development" while creating the identities of its subjects -- in this case, the "developed" First World/Tier and "undeveloped" Africa.[32] The development discourse of economic liberalism espoused by the international lending institutions -- the IMF and World Bank -- has been the dominant discourse in the late 20th century.

This development discourse has manifested itself in the institutions' Structural Adjustment Programs (SAPs), destabilization policies and free market rhetoric. What is significant for this essay is the recent inclusion of political conditionalities in the formulation of SAPs. The inclusion of political conditionalities reflects the seeming convergence of the two discourses -- democratization and development. What has actually happened, in fact, is the subordination of democracy to development.

Despite the rhetoric, international lending agencies are not interested in the creation of pluralist polities in Africa. Rather, they are concerned first and foremost with the realization of the goals of economic liberalism, as reflected in the second paradox mentioned above: democratization does not necessarily mean democracy. Claude Ake has argued that the international lending agencies have become so fixated on SAPs and the development discourse they will accept and protect any regime that follows it. What this has frequently meant is that African leaders have been able to substitute adherence to the development/ democratization discourse while avoiding any substantial democratic reforms.[33]

In order to overcome domestic obstacles, the implementation of SAPs requires authoritarian politics. Such moves increase the militarization of African societies while deepening divisions within those societies. Thus, the development discourse requires the de-democratization of African politics. Ake concludes that the external development agencies have felt constrained to give market reform priority over democracy. As the Zambia case illustrates, external interests defeat democracy, resulting in the exercising of power with out responsibility.[34]

The Democracy Discourse And The Example Of Mozambique

Perhaps no other example captures the power and paradoxes of the democratization discourse better than Mozambique. After waging a successful war for independence against the Portuguese, the Marxist-oriented FRELIMO [the Front for the Liberation of Mozambique] became the ruling government in 1975. The apartheid regime in South Africa and its surrogate RENAMO [Mozambique National Resistance] -- as well as the government's own misguided policies -- destabilized Mozambique's economy, however, and it began to collapse by the mid-1980s.[35] Realizing that it desperately needed Western aid and credit, Mozambique altered its Socialist rhetoric and joined the World Bank and the IMF in 1984.[36] By 1987, it was implementing its first IMF-sponsored Structural Adjustment Program. In the following years, Mozambique became a "model citizens" of the IMF, quickly adopting every policy and conditionality put forth by the lending agencies. The "good behavior" of Mozambique should not be too surprising considering that it is both the world's poorest and most heavily indebted country. The World Bank reported that Mozambique's GNP per capita was approximately $90 in 1993.[37] The depth and breadth of Mozambique's debt burden has been well documented elsewhere.[38] My purpose here is to note the level of dependency on the Western lending agencies. The growing leverage of the international lending agencies strengthened their insistence that Mozambique move to a market-oriented multi-party political system, reflecting the view that socialism and "democracy" or "development" are incompatible.

The collapse of the economy and the intractable civil war slowly convinced elements within the FRELIMO regime that changes needed to be made. On 17 July 1989, President Joaquim Chissano announced that the government was willing to enter into peace negotiations with RENAMO. During the Fifth Party Congress, held in July 1989, other radical changes were made. Most notable was the FRELIMO's rejection of Marxist-Leninism. The Congress produced a draft of a new constitution, officially unveiled on 9 January 1990, which allowed for a multi-party "democratic" political system. The final draft of the constitution was officially adopted on 30 November 1990. The Rome peace talks between the government and the rebels were remarkably successful, especially in the light of the collapse of the peace settlement in Angola. The country's first democratic elections were held in October 1994. President Chissano won 53.30% of the Presidential vote and FRELIMO was able to garner a very slim majority in the National Assembly.[39]

Yet, I am less concerned with the fact that FRELIMO held multi-party elections, than I am with questions of how democracy was conceived and practiced. Popular participation and involvement, as practiced by the Socialist regime, was determined to be illegitimate by the dominant "democracy discourse." To be legitimate meant that the political system had to be constructed around accepted, multi-party structures. Popular participation was less important than the existence of "legitimate" structures and institutions. Not surprisingly, one can observe that the current Mozambican political institutions are largely imitations of Western systems.[40]

Moreover, the international donor agents played an overt and significant role in defining and delineating Mozambique's democratization. For example, certain Constitutional provisions and legislative policies that were supported by various donor agencies were adopted despite resistance by the majority of FRELIMO, which held nation-wide debates on the proposed Constitution.[41] In numerous cases, Western lending agencies have used aid conditionalities to transform and limit a number of Mozambique's political and economic institutions. As for the loss of autonomy and sovereignty, a telling comment was made by President Chissano in 1990:

The U.S. said, "Open yourself to OPIC, the World Bank, and the IMF". What happened?... We are told now: "Marxism! You are devils. Change this policy." OK. Marxism is gone. "Open the market economy." OK, FRELIMO is trying to create capitalism... We went to Reagan and I said, "I want money for the private sector..." Answer: $10 million, then $15 million more, then another $15 million... OK we have changed... Now they say, "If you don't go to a multiparty system, don't expect help from us."[42]

On one hand, such a statement can be seen as propagandist political maneuvering. However, Cameron Hume, the US representative to the Rome peace talks, is equally frank in his discussion of how the US and its allies used their aid leverage to force FRELIMO to make concessions. This practice included using relief aid as a bargaining chip during the drought of 1991-92.[43] It should be remembered that during the late 1980s and early 1990s, Mozambique was both the poorest country in the world and the most aid dependent.[44] This relationship of dependency has resulted in the loss of sovereignty and autonomy of the Mozambican state. David Plank has argued that there now exists a "re-colonization" of Mozambique due to its aid dependence on donor agencies. He notes that while the relationship between the two is less overtly intrusive than direct colonialism was, its effects are considerably more pervasive. Further, Plank notes that the re-colonial relationship being established is potentially more durable because Mozambique's subordinate status is rooted in the widely accepted precepts of modern economic and democratic orthodoxy, not in flimsy claims of racial superiority or spiritual salvation that characterized earlier imperialism.

Finally, Plank notes that the lending agents have considerably more autonomy and authority over Mozambique than the Portuguese ever had, because Mozambique is more dependent on them than they were on Lisbon.[45] FRELIMO's almost unquestioning acceptance of the Western development and democratization discourse is often cited as evidence of dependency and the loss of Mozambican agency.[46] Yet, FRELIMO really has no choice: given the weight of their debt and the collapse of the bipolar international system, no viable aid alternatives exists, and alternative development and democratization discourses have been delegitimized.

In Peace Without Profit, Joseph Hanlon suggests possible alternative strategies and policies for Mozambique, such as emulating rural co-operatives, writing off the country's debt and raising the salaries of government officials operating a more interventionist state which adopts 'trickle-up' approaches to economic growth.[47] Yet, these policies are in direct conflict with the dominant development and democratization discourses.

As the World Bank and IMF enlarged the scope of their conditionalities beyond economic policies, the sovereignty of the Mozambican state has further diminished. The Mozambican state exists only to the extent that the Western lending agencies allow it to exist. As Mozambique's sovereignty is undercut, so too is its agency.

As David Plank observed, "public officials now have little choice but to do whatever the aid agencies demand of them."[48] Tom Young notes that "despite equipping Mozambique with all the trappings of a democratic state, the sheer leverage of outside powers, and in particular the coordinating role of the IMF/World Bank, have subjected Mozambique to an extraordinary degree of foreign tutelage.

Indeed, Mozambique has been made into a virtual laboratory for new forms of Western domination."[49] As the World Bank itself admits, "partly by design, partly by default, the Bank today has a near-monopoly on development strategy dialogue with the [Mozambican] Government."[50] There is, however, an interesting paradox. While the lending agencies are undercutting the sovereignty of the Mozambican state, they must increasingly rely on the continued existence of the state.   At one level, the lending agencies need the state for its repressive capability. A strong hand is necessary to ensure the implementation of the often harsh "medicine" of structural adjustment.

The lending agencies at the same time rely upon the existence of state institutions to provide the facade to legitimate the agencies' work within a country. So while the activities of lending agencies further crumble the state, their long-term goals rely on the continued existence of a state. Yet, the Western lending agencies are using conditionalities and influence to construct political institutions that serve their interests rather than the interests of the Mozambican society. As David Plank argued:
the donors have resumed trying to establish governments in Africa that are dedicated to the principles of efficiency, probity, and subsidiarity, whose policy choices will be determined by the same technocratic criteria as those that guide the aid agencies themselves... At the heart of this strategy is the creation of interlocutors for the aid agencies themselves.[51]

Thus, the resulting Mozambican state is "technically competent, economically rational, and politically dispassionate."[52] Significantly, the state has become an extension of the aid agencies rather than of the electorate. This is a chilling example of Claude Ake's observation that the development discourse requires the de-democratization of African societies.[53]

Conclusions

The arguments in this essay provide us more with questions than answers. But these are important new questions to ask. First, it is important to delineate which forces within the international society produce and employ these discourses. The "West" is not a monolithic entity. Attention should be paid to the specific forces involved in the production of these discourses. Whose interests are being served and to what ends? What is being gained by each discourse? How are these discourses transmitted through hegemonic international institutions? How do these institution's own agendas affect the reproduction and employment of these discourses?

Similarly, what roles do African elites play in the maintenance and practice of these discourses? By delineating the forces and practices involved in the production of these discourses, possibilities for resistance appear. In examining the discursive production of "democracy" and "development", care should be given to illuminating possible counter-hegemonic positions and paths. Questions should also be asked about the role of scholarship in the production of these discourses -- hegemonic and counter-hegemonic.

Given the argument that "democratization discourse" is linked to the Western discourse on development, the evolution of these discourses and their connection need to be closely historicized. Attention should also be paid to the ways in which these discourses are linked. Has the democracy/development distinction collapsed? Has development completely eclipsed democratization? Are these connections specific to certain contexts? What role has language played in this connection? The development discourse is often couched in evolutionary terminology. How have similar linguistic practices been employed in the discourse on democratization?

In addition to democratization and development, are there other discourses converging in the international community? Why and to what ends? Furthermore, considerable work is needed on the connection between the democracy and development discourses and the global capitalist division of labor. How and why are these discourses and identities necessary for the continuation of the capitalist world system? How have specific representations of African identities affected international relations? Considerably more empirical research needs to be done on the representation of African identities within the international community.[54]

What are the interests being served by the representations of Africans as "knowable" subjects? To what ends? How have these representations evolved over time? How have these identities allowed or justified certain courses of action -- from colonization to humanitarian intervention? What roles do Africans have in their own representation? How can new identities be formed to contest existing, Western-constructed representations? What should those new identities be?

The reader should not conclude that African societies are incapable of defining and traversing their own paths of "democratization." What this essay has tried to illustrate are the powerful forces that exist within international society that restrict the "legitimate" options available. The task before African societies is to define and pursue alternative paths outside the prevailing "democratic discourse." As Roxanne Lynn Doty notes, a discourse is inherently open-ended and incomplete, while "Hegemonic practices are those practices that seek to create the fixedness of meaning."[55]

One of the tasks before us is to challenge the existing, hegemonic democratization discourse. This challenge is particularly important for African societies, because this discourse reflects and perpetuates social identities and an international community based on an exploitative global economic division of labor. Discourses of democracy and development need to be broadened to include African experiences, perspectives and interests.[56]

The hegemonically-produced discourse of democracy -- like the development discourse -- serves to perpetuate an international society that is detrimental to both the development and democratization of African societies. Within these discourses are embedded important representational practices that construct international identities. These practices "enable one to 'know' and to act upon what one 'knows.'"[57]

Just as the dominant democratization and development discourses must be challenged, so too must the dominant representations of Africa and Africans which help legitimate these discourses even further.

The task is difficult, but not insurmountable.

NOTES

1. *Author's note*: I would like to thank Anna Creadick and Jasper Dunn for their critique, support and assistance. Thanks are also due to Edouard Bustin, Sheila Smith, Haco Hoang, Catherine White, Richard Joseph, Timothy Docking, Robert Art, James Der Derian, J.H. Proctor and Naeem Inayatullah for their support and inspiration.

2. Samuel huntington, *The Third Wave: Democratization in the Late Twentieth Century*, (Norman,OK:

University of Oklahoma Press, 1991.

3. See for instance: Marina Ottaway(ed),*Democracy in Africa: The Hard Road Ahead,*(boulder,CO: Lynne Rienner, 1997) and Richard Joseph (ed), *State. Conflict and Democracy in Africa* (boulder, CO: Lynne Rienner, 1998)

4. John Storey, *An Introduction Guide to Cultural Theory and Popular Culture*, Athens: University of Georgia Press. 1993. 91-92.

5. Roxanne Lynn Doty, *Imperial Encounters: The Politics of Representation in North-South Relations*, Minneapolis: University of Minnesota. 1996: 6.

6. Doty, 1996: 6.

7. Jan Nederveen Pieterse, *White on Black: Images of Africa and Blacks in Western Popular Culture*, New Haven: Yale University Press. 1992.

8. Thomas Biersteker and Cynthia Weber (eds.), *State Sovereignty as Social Construct*, Cambridge: Cambridge University Press. 1996.

9. Hedley Bull, *The Anarchical Society,* New York: Columbia University Press. 1977; Barry Buzan, "From International System to International Society: Structural Realism and Regime Theory Meet The English School" *International Organization,* 1993; Adam Watson, *The Evolution of International Society,* London: Routledge. 1992.

10. Basil Davidson, *The Black Man's Burden: Africa and the Curse of the Nation-State*, New York: Times Books. 1992.

11. Walter Rodney, *How Europe Underdeveloped Africa* revised. Washington: Howard University Press. 1981; Samir Amin, *Neo-Colonialism in West Africa*, New York: Monthly Review Press; Naeem Inayatullah "Beyond the sovereignty dilemma:

quasi-states as social construct" in Biersteker and Weber (eds.) *State Sovereignty as Social Construct*, Cambridge: Cambridge University Press. 1996.

12. Robert Cox, "Gramsci, Hegemony and Intl Relations: an essay in method" in Gill (ed.), *Gramsci, Historical Materialism and International Relations,* Cambridge: Cambridge University Press. 1993: 61.

13. Cox, 1993: 62.

14. Buzan, 1993

15. Robert Jackson and Carl Rosberg, "Why Africa's Weak States Persist: The Empirical and the Juridical in Statehood" *World Politics*. 1982.

16. Jackson and Rosberg, 1982

17. Buzan, 1993: 345.

18. Several points should be made with regards to my use of the concept of identity. First, identities are socially constructed. The characteristics, meanings and boundaries of identities are not natural or universal, but emerge within the play of specific social forces. Identities are malleable, rather than fixed and static. Second, identities are not singular or unitary. The characteristics, meanings and boundaries of identity are always up for grabs. Attempts at strict definition and refection are, therefore, power practices. Third, identities are historically specific. Identities, their meanings, characteristics and boundaries, shift over time in the face of contestation. Fourth, identities are discursively produced. They are to be found in language and images, representations and characterizations. See Stuart Hall, Who Needs Identity=? in S. Hall and P. Du Gay (eds) *Questions of Cultural Identity*. London: Sage. 1996.

19. Yosef Lapid and Friedrich Kratochwil (eds.), *The Return of Culture and Identity in IR Theory*, Boulder: Lynne Rienner. 1996; David Campbell, *Writing Security: United States Foreign Policy and the Politics of Identity*, Minneapolis: University of Minnesota. 1992; Cynthia Weber, Writing Sovereign Identities *Alternatives*. (17:3). 1992; Alexander Wendt,"The Agent-Structure Problem in International Relations Theory" *International Organization*, (41) 1987; Alexander Wendt, "Anarchy is What States Make of It; The Social Construction of Power Politics" *International Organization*, (46,2) 1992; Alexander Wendt, Identity and Structural Change in International Politics in Lapid and Kratochwil (ed). *The Return of Culture and Identity in IR Theory*, Boulder: Lynne Rienner. 1996; Marysia Zalewski and Cynthia Enloe, A Questions about Identity in International Relations@ in Booth and Smith (eds.), *International Relations Theory Today*, 1995.,Waever, O., Buzan, B., Kelstrup, M. and Lemaitre, P., *Identity, Migration and the New Security Agenda in Europe*, London: Frances Pinter. 1993. p.5.

20. Zalewski and Enloe, 1995.

21. Roxanne Lynn Doty, "Foreign Policy as Social Construction: A Post-Positivist Analysis of U.S. Counterinsurgency Policy in the Philippines" *International Studies Quarterly*, (37) 1993.

22. Doty, 1996; Tzvetan Todorov, *The Conquest of America: The Question of the Other*, New York: Harper and Row. 1984.

23. See Inayatullah, 1996; Kevin Dunn, "Constructing Africa: Representation, Identity, and International Relations," Northeast International Studies Association

Conference, Philadelphia, Nov. 1997.

24. Doty, 1996: 13.

25. Doty, 1996: 13.

26. For examples of these Western conceptions of democracy, see Robert Dahl, *A Preface to Democratic Theory*. Chicago: University of Chicago. 1956; Anthony Downs, *An Economic Theory of Democracy*. New York: Harper. 1957; Larry Diamond and Plattner (eds.), *The Global Resurgence of Democracy*. Baltimore: John Hopkins. 1993; and Huntington, 1991.

27. Donald Snow and Eugene Brown, *The Contours of Power: An Introduction to Contemporary International Relations,* New York: St. Martin's. 1996.

28.. Freedom House, *Freedom in the World: The Annual Survey of Political Rights and Civil Liberties 1994-1995*, New York: Freedom House. 1995: 5.

29. Carol Lancaster, *United States and Africa: Into the Twenty-First Century Policy Essay No. 7*, Washington: Overseas Development Council. 1993: 27.

30. Alternative democratic discourses certainly exist. For example, see Cjlestin Monga, "Measuring Democracy: A Comparative Theory of Political Well-Being, " Boston University African Studies Center Working Paper No. 206, 1996; Ernesto Laclau and Chantal Mouffe, *Hegemony and Socialist Strategy: Toward a Radical Democratic Politics*. London: Verso. 1985.

31. James Ferguson, *The Anti-Politics Machine: "Development,"Depoliticization , and Bureaucratic Power in Lesotho*. Minneapolis: University of Minnesota. 1994.

32. See also Doty, 1996.

33. Claude Ake "Rethinking African Democracy" in Diamond and Plattner (eds.) *The_Global Resurgence of Democracy*, Baltimore: John Hopkins University Press. 1993: 120.

34. Ake, 1996.

35. Merle Bowen, "Beyond Reform: Adjustment and Political Power in Contemporary Mozambique *Journal of Modern African Studies* (30:2) 1992; Joseph Hanlon, *Beggar Your Neighbors: Apartheid Power in Southern Africa* . Bloomington: Indiana University. 1986; Joseph Hanlon , *Mozambique: Who Calls the Shots?* London: James Currey. 1991; Plank, David N. "Aid, Debt, and the End of Sovereignty: Mozambique and Its Donors" *Journal of Modern African Studies* (31:3) 1993; Barry Schultz, "The Heritage of Revolution and the Struggle for Governmental Legitimacy in Mozambique" in Zartman (ed) *Collapsed States: The Disintegration and Restoration of Legitimate Authority*. Boulder: Lynne Reinner. 1995; and Mark Simpson, "Foreign and Domestic Factors in the Transformation of Frelimo" *Journal of Modern African Studies* (31:2) 1993.

36. Marina Ottaway. "Mozambique: From Symbolic Socialism to Symbolic Reform." *Journal of Modern African Studies*. (26) 1988: 211-226.

37. World Bank. *World Development Report 1995: Workers in an Integrated World*. Oxford: Oxford University Press. 1995: 162.

38. Chris Alden and Mark Simpson , "Mozambique: a Delicate Peace" *The Journal of Modern African Studies* (31:1) 1993; Chris Alden, "The UN and the Resolution of Conflict in Mozambique" *The Journal of Modern African Studies* (33:1) 1995; Hanlon, 1991; Bowen, 1992; Plank, 1993; and Simpson, 1993.

39. Schultz, 1995; Hanlon, 1996.

40. Tim Docking and Kevin Dunn. "Imitation and Innovation: The Construction of Democracy in Mali and Mozambique," Paper presented at the GRAF Research Conference "L'Afrique, Les Etats-Unis et la France," University of Bordeaux, France, May 1997.

41. Bowen, 1992; Simpson, 1993.

42. Quoted in John Saul, "Mozambique: the failure of socialism?" *Southern Africa Report* (6) 1990: 21.
43. Cameron Hume, *Ending Mozambique's War: The Role of Mediation and Good Offices,* Washington: U.S. Institute of Peace. 1994.: 97-8.

44. See Hanlon, 1991; Bowen, 1992; Plank, 1993; Simpson, 1993; Alden and Simpson, 1993; Alden, 1995; World Bank, 1995; Hanlon, 1996.

45. Plank, 1993: 428-29.

46. Bowen, 1992; Plank, 1993; Hanlon, 1991; Hanlon, 1996.

47. Hanlon, 1996: 84-149.

48. Plank, 1993: 417.

49. Tom Young, "'A Project to be Realised': Global Liberalism and Contemporary Africa" *Millennium* (24:2) 1995: 542.

50. Quoted in Young, 1995: 538-39.

51. Plank, 1993: 425.

52. Plank, 1993: 426.

53. Ake, 1996.

54. See Kevin Dunn, *The Politics of Identity in Central Africa: Power, Representation and International Relations,* forthcoming.

55. Doty 1996: 8; see also Ernesto Laclau and Chantal Mouffe, *Hegemony and Socialist Strategy: Towards a Radical Democratic Politics.* London: Verso. 1985: 112.

56. See for example Monga, 1996; Ake, 1996.

20 *Contemporary African Politics*

Bibliography

Ake, Claude, Democracy and Development in Africa, Washington: The Brookings Institute. 1996.

Ake, Claude, "Rethinking African Democracy" in Diamond and Plattner (eds.), The Global Resurgence of Democracy, Baltimore: John Hopkins University Press. 1993.

Alden, Chris and Mark Simpson, "Mozambique: a Delicate Peace" *Journal of Modern African Studies* (31:1) 1993.

Alden, Chris, "The UN and the Resolution of Conflict in Mozambique" *Journal of Modern African Studies* (33:1) 1995.

Amin, Samir, Neo-Colonialism in West Africa, New York: Monthly Review Press. 1973.

Biersteker, Thomas and Cynthia Weber (eds.), State Sovereignty as Social Construct, Cambridge: Cambridge University Press. 1996.

Bowen, Merle, "Beyond Reform: Adjustment and Political Power in Contemporary Mozambique" *Journal of Modern African Studies* (30:2) 1992.

Bull, Hedley, The Anarchical Society, New York: Columbia University Press. 1977.

Buzan, Barry, "From International System to International Society: Structural Realism and Regime Theory Meet The English School" International Organization, 1993.

Campbell, David, Writing Security: United States Foreign Policy and the Politics of Identity, Minneapolis: University of Minnesota. 1992.

Cox, Robert, "Gramsci, Hegemony and Intl Relations: an essay in method" in Gill (ed.), Gramsci, Historical Materialism and International Relations, Cambridge: Cambridge University Press. 1993.

Dahl, Robert, A Preface to Democratic Theory, Chicago: University of Chicago Press. 1956.

Davidson, Basil, The Black Man's Burden: Africa and the Curse of the Nation-State, New York: Times Books. 1992.

Diamond, Larry and Mark Plattner (eds.), The Global Resurgence of Democracy, Baltimore: John Hopkins. 1993.

Docking, Tim and Kevin Dunn. "Imitation and Innovation: The Construction of Democracy in Mali and Mozambique," Paper presented at the GRAF Research Conference "L'Afrique, Les Etats-Unis et la France," University of Bordeaux, France, May 1997.

Doty, Roxanne Lynn, "Foreign Policy as Social Construction: A Post-Positivist Analysis of U.S. Counterinsurgency Policy in the Philippines" International Studies Quarterly, (37), 1993.

Doty, Roxanne Lynn, Imperial Encounters: The Politics of Representation in North-South Relations, Minneapolis: University of Minnesota. 1996.

Downs, Anthony, An Economic Theory of Democracy, New York: Harper. 1957.

Dunn, Kevin, "Constructing Africa: Representation, Identity, and International Relations," Northeast International Studies Association Conference, Philadelphia, Nov. 1997.

Ferguson, James, The Anti-Politics Machine: "Development," Depoliticization, and Bureaucratic Power in Lesotho, Minneapolis: University of Minnesota. 1994.

Freedom House, Freedom in the World: The Annual Survey of Political Rights and Civil Liberties 1994-1995, New York: Freedom House. 1995.

Hall, Stuart, "Who Needs Identity ?" in S. Hall and P. Du Gay (eds.), Questions of Cultural Identity, London: Sage. 1996.

Hanlon, Joseph, Beggar Your Neighbors: Apartheid Power in Southern Africa, Bloomington: Indiana University. 1986.

Hanlon, Joseph, Mozambique: Who Calls the Shots?, London: James Currey. 1991.

Hume, Cameron, Ending Mozambique's War: The Role of Mediation and Good Offices, Washington: U.S. Institute of Peace. 1994.

Huntington, Samuel, The Third Wave: Democratization in the Late Twentieth Century, University of Oklahoma Press, 1991.

Inayatullah, Naeem, "Beyond the sovereignty dilemma: quasi-states as social construct" in Biersteker and Weber (eds.), State Sovereignty as Social Construct, Cambridge: Cambridge University Press. 1996.

Jackson, Robert and Carl Rosberg, "Why Africa's Weak States Persist: The Empirical and the Juridical in Statehood" World Politics. 1982.

Joseph, Richard (ed.), State, Conflict, and Democracy in Africa, Boulder: Lynn Rienner. 1998.

Laclau, Ernesto and Chantal Mouffe, Hegemony and Socialist Strategy: Towards a Radical Democratic Politics, London: Verso. 1985.

Lancaster, Carol, United States and Africa: Into the Twenty-First Century. Policy essay No. 7, Washington: Overseas Development Council. 1993.

Lapid, Yosef and Friedrich Kratochwil (eds.), The Return of Culture and Identity in IR Theory, Boulder: Lynne Rienner. 1996.

Monga, CJlestin, "Measuring Democracy: A Comparative Theory of Political Well-Being," Boston University African Studies Center Working Paper No. 206, 1996.

Nederveen Pieterse, Jan, White on Black: Images of Africa and Blacks in Western Popular Culture, New Haven: Yale University Press. 1992.

Ottaway, Marina (ed.), Democracy in Africa: The Hard Road Ahead, Boulder: Lynn Rienner. 1997.

Ottaway, Marina, "Mozambique: From Symbolic Socialism to Symbolic Reform" Journal of Modern African Studies, (26) 1988.

Plank, David N. "Aid, Debt, and the End of Sovereignty: Mozambique and Its Donors" *Journal of Modern African Studies* (31:3) 1993.

Rodney, Walter, How Europe Underdeveloped Africa revised, Washington: Howard University Press. 1981.

Saul, John. "Mozambique: the failure of socialism?" *Southern Africa Report* (6) 1990.

Schultz, Barry, "The Heritage of Revolution and the Struggle for Governmental Legitimacy in Mozambique" in Zartman (ed.), Collapsed States: The Disintegration and Restoration of Legitimate Authority, Boulder: Lynne Reinner. 1995.

Simpson, Mark, "Foreign and Domestic Factors in the Transformation of Frelimo" *Journal of Modern African Studies* (31:2) 1993.

Snow, Donald and Eugene Brown, The Contours of Power: An Introduction to Contemporary International Relations, New York: St. Martin's. 1996.

Storey, John, An Introduction Guide to Cultural Theory and Popular Culture, Athens: University of Georgia Press. 1993.

Todorov, Tzvetan, The Conquest of America: The Question of the Other, New York: Harper and Row. 1984.

Waever, O., Buzan, B., Kelstrup, M. and Lemaitre, P., Identity, Migration and the New Security Agenda in Europe, London: Frances Pinter. 1993.

Watson, Adam, The Evolution of International Society, London: Routledge. 1992.

Weber, Cynthia, "Writing Sovereign Identities" *Alternatives.* (17:3). 1992.

Wendt, Alexander, "Identity and Structural Change in International Politics" in Lapid and Kratochwil (ed.), The Return of Culture and Identity in IR Theory, Boulder: Lynne Rienner. 1996.

Wendt, Alexander, "Anarchy is What States Make of It: The Social Construction of Power Politics" International Organization. (46). 1992.

Wendt, Alexander,"The Agent-Structure Problem in International Relations Theory" International Organization. (41). 1987.

World Bank, World Development Report 1995: Workers in an Integrated World, Oxford: Oxford University Press. 1995.

Young, Tom, "'A Project to be Realised': Global Liberalism and Contemporary Africa" *Millennium* (24:2) 1995.

Zalewski, Marysia and Cynthia Enloe, " Questions about Identity in International Relations" in Booth and Smith (eds.), International Relations Theory Today, 1995.

Chapter 2

International Efforts At Democracy And Sub-Saharan Africa Development.

Adegboyega A. Somide

This chapter examines the contradictory objectives of the various international and local actors attempting to promote political and economic liberalization in sub-Saharan Africa since 1980. It concludes that while there appears to be a coherent policy among international actors such as the international financial institutions and the Western aid donors, there are important divergences among them. And, more importantly, there are significant differences between them and the local African people. These differences constitute a major obstacle to any successful transition to market-led economies and democracy.

Introduction:

Since the early 1980s, and with increasing urgency after the breakdown of the communist structure in Eastern Europe and the former Soviet Union, regimes in sub-Saharan Africa (SSA) have been under tremendous international pressures to establish market-led economies and democratic governance. More than any time since independence almost four decades ago, international policy responses to SSA political and economic crises were seemingly coordinated. The pressures on SSA regimes to liberalize their political and economic systems emanated from three distinct international sources: 1)the Bretton Woods Institutions (BWIs); 2) Western aid donors; and 3)various agencies of the United Nations. There was an implicit assumption by these actors that a simultaneous pursuit of economic and political liberalization would ameliorate Africa's economic and political woes, thus launching it on a development course experienced by key Western industrial democracies.

Based on policy statements by the United States, the World Bank and the IMF, this study assumes that development is, at least, a part of the reason for the current push for economic and political liberalization. Therefore, liberal capitalist democracy is the independent variable while development is the dependent variable. Because the independent variable has two components, economic and political, I assess the degree to which the dependent variable is affected by variations of either the economic or political dimension of liberal capitalist democracy. In other words, if a country liberalizes its political system but actively intervenes in the economy, what are the consequences for development? Conversely, how is development affected in a country that combines free market system with authoritarianism? I will attempt to answer these questions by examining the policies of the BWIs in SSA.

I will also assess whether parallel political and economic liberalization has resulted in democratic consolidation in SSA. I will evaluate the compatibility of these goals, the instruments mustered in their pursuit, and the results of democracy promotion in SSA since 1980. Early international efforts to democratize the political and economic systems of African states were piecemeal. The containment of communism was considered to be far more important, and many African dictators were considered Western allies in this regard. By 1989, the collapse of Soviet-sponsored communism effectively removed the leverage hitherto enjoyed by African authoritarian regimes. This allowed Western-dominated International Financial Institutions (IFIs) to pursue the goal of economic and political liberalization more vigorously.

The inclusion of political conditionality in the BWIs' lending policies signified the beginning of a new era in democracy promotion in Africa. I argue that irrespective of the wave of political and economic liberalization which began in 1991, the use of economic inducements to nudge SAA authoritarian regimes toward democracy has not produced the desired results. Part I provides a brief historical background by discussing the colonial legacy and the failure of democratic institutions in post-colonial SSA. Part II examines theoretical perspectives on development. Part III discusses actors, methods and results. It explores the issue of why the BWIs policy changed toward Africa in the late 1980s and whether or not this has been successful. Parts IV and V explore possible international and African factors mitigating against democracy.

Definitions and Concepts

Democracy has been defined in a variety of manners, depending on the motive and the purpose for which the definition is intended. Thus, there is talk of a Russian, Asian or African democracy that is presumably different from the Western conceptualization of democracy. Some definitions stress substantive qualities, while others amplify procedural ones. Still others insist on a stringent combination of both. In this study, I use the term democracy to denote a political system in which the following basic procedural conditions have been met: 1) Free and fair elections occur at regular intervals as the method of selecting the most important officials in government; 2) competition for political offices is open to all individuals and organized groups with no part of society denied participation; and 3) the existence of sufficient levels of civil and political liberties that afford individuals and groups the freedom to express their opinions, assemble and organize electoral campaign without being harassed, intimidated or censored.

This definition emphasizes political participation and governmental accountability. Tolerance of opposition and protection of human and civil rights, as often enshrined in a constitution, must be respected for the abilities and resources of a society to be fully mobilized for development. The term "development," as used in this study, eschews the typical adjunct status which assigns it to the end of other adjectives such as political, economic or social. Here, "development" refers to what Gerald Meier describes as the "upward movement of the entire social system."

According to this definition, development has both quantitative and qualitative dimensions that include: (1) greater capacity to improve the performance of factors of production through the use of technology. (2) industrial expansion (3) increased institutional capabilities and a change in attitudes and values (4) social and economic equalization, and (5) greater ability to cope with nature and "undesirable conditions in the social system that have perpetuated a state of underdevelopment."

By adopting Meier's elements of development, I emphasize the importance of investment in the necessary production and technology that will ensure efficient production and distribution of material resources and greater ability to cope with nature. Conceived in this way, development entails society's realization of a better quality of life for the general populace and the removal of conditions that promote income disparity by favoring one class over the other.

Thus, solutions to a society's development do not merely involve economic and political choices at the top. Nor can they be induced by macroeconomic adjustments alone. I argue that development is a process that can only be attained and sustained with the involvement of the masses. Hence, democracy is both a requisite and a product of development. The conception of development held by some key economists of the post-World War II era, e.g. Walt W. Rostow (and still held by some, e.g. Anne O. Krueger) differs from the above definition in that it tends to emphasize aggregate rates of growth. In the same vein, political scientists motivated by Cold War considerations tended to advocate Western-style democracy. I shall have more to say on this in part II.

One must be careful in predicting democracy's relationship to development. The conception of development in this paper makes it integral to democracy. Yet, when touted by development agencies as a means of social change and/or progress, as an imitation of Western values and mores, it probably will fail. Western societies are radically different from African societies. If liberal representative democracy developed in the West following industrial capitalism, what are the prospects for its development in largely pre-capitalist societies? For this reason and others, many Africans, while not arguing with the IFIs or donor nations who hold out liberal capitalist democracy as the key to African development, question their motivation and sincerity.

The perceptions, expectations and attitudes of outsiders and the local population involved in political and economic liberalization are of great importance in determining the success or failure of transition. Democracy as defined above reinforces and, indeed, is indispensable for development. Ideally, the objectives of international development agencies must mesh with one another and with those of the local people, and means to realize those objectives must not be associated with negative results. For example, greater income disparities or deepening ethnic cleavages can replace transition with a reversal to authoritarianism. The issue of compatibility of goals is further discussed in part IV.

Africa's colonial legacy casts a long shadow on current efforts to promote democracy. Anyone seeking to understand the challenges of political change and economic development in SSA needs to grasp how SSA states came into existence in the first place. In the post-independence era, African regimes have been suspicious of foreign intervention and quick to level charges of neocolonialism. The xenophobic proclivity is exemplified by some African regimes who view the IFIs and the Western donors' aid and loan conditionalities as unwelcome external intervention in

SSA domestic affairs reminiscent of colonial days.

PART I

Colonial Experience And Independence.

   The wounds from the slave trade from Africa to the "New World" marred the face of the African continent when an event of epochal significance occurred - namely, the direct political subjugation of the whole continent, except for Ethiopia. European relations with Africa had been dictated by commercial interests until the Franco-Prussian War of 1870-1871. Belching steam engines in Birmingham and other European industrial cities had corresponded with the rumble of earth in Africa as vital resources were extracted for machine lubrication and assorted manufactures.
   The European power balance, achieved after the defeat of Napoleon, became shaky. Germany had become powerful enough to cause jitters in Paris and London, and nationalism was becoming a potent force among the leading European countries jockeying for power. German annexation of French Alsace-Lorraine in 1871 had "inflamed French nationalism." But with nowhere to turn for self-assertion in contiguous Europe, France sought power and prestige in the acquisition of colonies in Africa and Asia.
   By 1884, it was clear that European commercial interests in Africa could easily escalate into another war, a war that Germany, given its preeminence in Europe, did not want, lest the power balance be altered to its disadvantage. Together with France, Bismarck called a conference of fourteen European powers in Berlin on 15 November 1884 to formulate "a set of rules defining the orderly extension of European influence in Africa". The Berlin Conference was unique in two significant respects. First, it was a conference on Africa but not by Africans. Second, the agenda of the meeting was unmistakably European interest. As Robert July aptly summed it up, at stake was "the delicate balance of power among European nations, the projection of their rising mercantile interests... and the nourishment of national pride which had recently begun to express itself through the acquisition of colonial territories".
   The partitioning of Africa meant that African boundaries were artificially drawn by European powers. In contemporary SSA, states are an amalgamation of numerous disparate ethnic groups with no historical, social, or political relations to one another. While their multi-ethnic composition does not necessarily portend disaster, the

nature of states in Africa has served to reinforce rather than diminish ethnic allegiances. This is crucial to the prospect of democratization, as elaborated in part V.

In many countries, the "wind of change" that blew across Africa in 1960 witnessed the installation of a new African ruler, elected according to democratic institutional practices of the departing colonial power. But in country after country, the new governments soon collapsed as ethnic strife and military coups and countercoups proliferated. Between 1960 and 1992, there were 61 successful military coups, and 10 countries experienced full-scale civil war. Most regimes, whether military, quasi-military or civilian, have since been "essentially undemocratic and hegemonial."

Post- Colonial Approaches to Development.

Most African leaders at independence simply reproduced the structure of the colonial state, deepening Africa's dependence on the metropolitan powers in the process. The retention of the colonial economic structure became an appealing option owing to what Claude Ake has described as "the dearth of ideas," "manpower constraints" and preoccupation with power consolidation. Western approaches to development were embraced as the solution to a myriad social, economic and political problems, even as Western potentates were rejected. In short, most initiatives for African development have come from the West, with only a few countries adopting the Marxist model.

For analytical purposes, Africa's post-independence development models can be divided into three general categories.
They are: 1) the capitalist state-interventionist model adopted, for instance, by Nigeria, Kenya, Cote d'Ivoire and Senegal; 2) African socialism which was popular in Tanzania and Guinea; and 3) the Marxist revolutionary model of Angola, Guinea-Bissau, and Mozambique.

The capitalist state-interventionist model uses the power of the state to bring about conditions favorable to the development of capitalism. Because the priority is to promote domestic capital accumulation, many of SSA countries using this model are often arrayed against foreign owners of businesses. In contrast, African Socialism is predicated on the assumption that African societies were naturally egalitarian and that class differentiation was imposed by capitalists. A return to African socialism and modernization can be achieved through a massive government-sponsored reorganization of peasants and workers.

The Marxist model has as its objective "a social revolution of the masses" to reinstate "a new humanist being who would restore and cultivate Africa's most valued cultural backgrounds of humanism." For many reasons, as discussed in part III, all three development models have largely failed. The capitalist-interventionist model often is said to have contributed to higher economic growth in the first two decades of independence, but the continent-wide economic crises of the 1970s, widening income gap and declining living standard have largely offset the initial gains.

The reality in Africa is that most regimes avoid extreme positions and blend *laissez-faire* with active government intervention. Thus, mixed-economy is a more appropriate characterization. For instance, in essentially capitalist countries such as Nigeria and Zaire, the recognition of market failure possibilities and concern with equity are important justifications for government ownership of production and indigenization programs.

It is almost 40 years since most African states gained their independence. Much of the euphoria that accompanied those momentous events has receded in the face of intractable political and economic woes. The world has watched in dismay as military coups and counter-coups engulfed the continent. Where military intervention had been averted, a brand of authoritarian single-party system emerged.

The unworkability of Western political institutions in Africa became evident when, in the first few years of independence, political and ethnic conflicts proved unresolvable within Western institutional frameworks.

This was not really surprising. First, the colonial state was anything but democratic. Second, its absolute and arbitrary power precluded any popular participation or community role in the political affairs. Having been schooled under such a centralized system, African elites had come to view the accumulation of political power as the only means to security. In post-independence Africa, politics was a zero-sum-game and norms and values of compromise, constraints and accountability were largely absent. A politician became synonymous with an ethnic entrepreneur. It was little wonder that ethnic groups were obsessed by the pursuit of political power.

PART II

Theoretical Perspectives On Development And Their Relevance In SSA

Two events of the post-World War II era influenced the direction of Western social science research and consequently the development paradigm foisted on Africa. These events are the proliferation of sovereign states in the former colonies of Asia and Africa and the advent of the Cold

War. The end of the war and the resultant division of the world into two ideological blocs, each headed by one of the two superpowers - the United States and the Soviet Union - marked the beginning of the Cold War. Subsequent rivalries between the two blocs encompassed socio-economic, politico-military, and cultural realms. Projection and expansion of influence in the emerging Third World countries thus became a key measure of superiority; thus the Third World became the theater where much of the Cold War battle was waged.

During the 1950s and 1960s, research on "political development" gained increasing popularity in the United States. According to Howard Wiarda, this could either be attributed to "U.S. Cold War strategies" to extend its economic and political systems to Third World countries or to a benign but naive and ethnocentric attempt by Western social scientists to guide development therein.

The torrent of literature on development during this period, coupled with the United States government's "development effort,"
demonstrated in such programs as the Peace Corps, the United States Agency for International Development (USAID), and increased development research funding, made the Cold War a more plausible explanation. In addition, the Anglo-American agreements at Bretton Woods in 1944 created an open international economic system and institutions that later set parameters for African development.

Development agencies, until recently, have tended to emphasize the economic dimensions of development, ignoring the social and political contexts in which economic activities take place. Conceived in this way, development need only be concerned with economic growth for which Gross National Product (GNP)per capita is a primary yardstick for success. In Africa, as with many Third World countries, development agenda has failed to factor in the social and political variables. This myopic view of development has resulted in a particular understanding of "success" by the BWIs that is at variance with expectations among Africans.

Consequently, many Third World investments have failed to address human welfare while actually increasing income disparities. The failure of GNP per capita as an accurate measure of economic development is best illustrated by the economies on Middle Eastern oil-producing nations. As pointed out by Hadjor, "Pure quantitative growth in and of itself does not produce development." While Saudi Arabia and Kuwait have very high GNP per capita, "wealth has remained in the hands of the elite and much of the country lives as before".

The studies of political development which appeared in the 1950s and

1960s assumed the universality and ineluctability of change. This tendency was rooted in the Greek philosophy of progress which was later propounded in the Western Enlightenment thoughts of Kant and Condorcet. Thus, there was an implicit assumption in the early theories of political development that the history of Western development is bound to be replicated in the non-Western societies. This assumption, unfortunately, informed and guided the activities of the international development agencies in Africa.

But the developmental thought of the 1950s and 60s differed from the progress theories in that it posited the ubiquity of social change. Societies were conceived as passing through social time that has a beginning but an "open-ended" future. Modernity was merely the most advanced pole that linked the present with the past and offered a glimpse of the future. As such, they abstracted stages, critical junctures, such as traditional, transitional, and modern. This was in marked contrast to the ancient progress theories in which "change is the growth of some desirable aspect of society (typically rational knowledge) and a concomitant zero-sum decline in its obverse (superstition or ignorance)".

There is now a consensus that the studies of "political development" in the 1950s and 1960s, (either the Parsonian systems perspective utilized in Gabriel Almond's *Politics of Developing Areas* or Samuel Huntington's *Political Order in Changing Societies*) were deterministic, in postulating that Western history would be replicated in societies that lacked "the sociopolitical precepts of Greece, Rome, and the Bible, without the same experience of feudalism and capitalism, and not having experienced the cultural history of the West." Political development theories of the 1950s consciously avoided political economy variables to inhere disciplinary autonomy and to avoid being labelled Marxist at the height of the Cold War ideological impasse.

In the 1970s, Marxist-inspired dependency theory appeared to argue that the persistence of underdevelopment together with myriad other social problems in the Third World resulted from unequal relations between the advanced capitalist countries and weak Third World countries. Because the capitalist system sought to maintain its dominance, its economic interests were often at variance with that of the Third World, resulting in the latter's perennial underdevelopment.

The political development approach posited the superiority of Western Enlightenment and its social and techo-scientific byproducts. It assumes that all societies will develop along path experienced by the West. Traditional societies are irrational and atavistic, and will soon disappear under the relentless assault of universal modernization and rationalization.

Both the developmental and the dependency paradigms have been discredited. In a critique of both paradigms, W. Rand Smith argued that the increasing interdependence of the global economy and a lack of any significant development in much of the Third World in the past two decades have meant that political variables alone are inadequate in explaining development. The dependency paradigm, on the other hand, has been undermined by "the emergence of several newly industrializing countries (NICs)," thus casting "doubt on the core-periphery dichotomy."

What should be noted here is that regardless of the conflicting paradigms, the setting of the African development agenda since independence has remained the preserve of external agencies. This fact needs to be emphasized, since it became a bone of contention between African governments and the international development community as African economies stagnated in the 1970s and 1980s.

PART III

The IMF, The World Bank And Aid Conditionality In SSA

My aim in this part is to examine the reasons behind the intensification of aid conditionality within the BWIs in the 1980s, and the convergence of roles, particularly the political dimension of conditionality, in SSA. A thorough study of the institutional history, the myriad programs and their indepth evaluation is beyond the scope of this study. What is of interest to us is the extent to which the programs of the BWIs have been compatible or contradictory with that of African countries. In addition, are the objectives of these programs conflicting with that of the other actors, for instance, the bilateral donors and NGOs.

The two BWIs were created at the Bretton Woods Conference in 1944 as specialized agencies of the United Nations. The IMF and the World Bank were originally created for different objectives. The World Bank, officially known as the International Bank for Reconstruction and Development, was to help reconstruct the devastated economies of Western Europe and Japan following World War II. Later, its domain was extended to the Third World. The biggest development bank in the world, the World Bank now has about 180 member-nations and provided about 20 billion dollars in 1996 for various development projects.

The IMF, in contrast to the World Bank, was designed to perform short-term credit operations to help rectify "balance of payments" difficulties of member nations. This is generally accomplished by providing short-term loans to be used for balance of payments corrections. The switch to floating exchange rates in the 1970s resulted in the adoption of new role by the Fund--the monitoring of exchange rates. Loan amounts depend on a member's special drawing rights (quotas) in the fund which is determined by one or any combination of factors ranging from "the country's national income, gold and foreign exchange reserves, size and fluctuations of its foreign trade, and export dependence." Members' quotas are divided into five *tranches*. One is held on deposit, while the Fund will lend against the other four if the Fund's conditions of stabilization are met. The quota system has ensured the dominance of Western powers in the Fund's operation. The United States alone controls about 20 percent of the fund and can use its voting power to push policies or block unwanted proposals.

Explaining The Expanding Role Of The BWIs

It is hardly a secret that virtually all SSA countries are confronted with serious political and economic crises. In the early 1970s, the neocolonial economic order began to crumble in SSA at the height of the global oil glut. The 1980s has often been referred to as the "lost decade" for SSA. The unprecedented decline in the per capita income of most Africans, the sharp decline in trade volume with the rest of the world, and the negligible foreign investment in SSA led to talk of Africa's "marginalization" in the world economy.

In order to understand Africa's crisis of the 1970s and 1980s, one must understand the nature of the neo-colonial economic order. As discussed in part II, all post-colonial African regimes were *dirigiste*, that is, the state actively directed the economy. The antecedent was the colonial economic structure where the state defined and regulated access to economic resources. This structure was adapted and developed into an elaborate patronage-based mode of production in the post-colonial era. A form of politicized accumulation which emerged under this clientelistic politics constrained the possibilities of capital expansion, retarded competitive capitalism and contributed to the collapse of many SSA economies.

This continental economic crisis prompted a series of conferences within the Organization of African Unity (OAU) and the United Nations Economic Commission for Africa (UNECA) throughout the 1970s, the outcome of which was a scathing indictment of the international economic structure for its part in Africa's underdevelopment. Not surprisingly, this open criticism of outside agents brought African governments in direct conflict with the BWIs which emphasized government mismanagement as the cause of Africa's economic problems. The controversy began with the adoption of *The Lagos Plan of Action* by African governments at the OAU summit at Lagos in April 1980.

The Lagos Plan of Action was audacious in two important respects. First, it implicated the BWIs' development strategies of the previous 20 years as having exacerbated Africa's social and economic crisis. Second, by proclaiming alternative strategies that would restructure Africa's economies through greater emphasis on self-reliance and self-sustaining development, the plan rejected the African role as producers of primary commodities in the existing international division of labor. The plan outlined measures that would break Africa's dependence on external forces by emphasizing collective self-reliance. That is, regional approach to industrialization, "a pooling of resources, and greater inter-African trade and cooperation."

In 1981, a report by the World Bank--*Accelerated Development*--presented a sharply divergent view of the causes of, and solution to, Africa's economic decline. It stressed internal factors such as "underdevelopment of human resources, climatic conditions and overproduction, and policy failures." As for solutions, it said African countries should rely more on market forces, eliminate public sector wastes and inefficiencies, and reform the "input supply and marketing services for the agricultural producers."

With their economies rapidly deteriorating in the mid-1980s, African countries capitulated to the World Bank views. Acutely aware of the power asymmetry, they sacrificed their convictions in Africa's Priority Program for Economic Recovery, 1986-1990 (APPER), a program of action contained in a document submitted at the United Nations special session on Africa's economic and social crisis in 1986. Unlike *The Lagos Plan of Action*, APPER now reflected the views expressed in *Accelerated Development*. It conceded that Africa was primarily responsible for its economic woes, not the international development agencies. It further substituted strengthening of the agricultural sector for economic restructuring and industrialization as the remedy for economic development and self-reliance.

In 1986, the United Nations published its own program for Africa's economic recovery called the United Nations Programme of Action for African Economic Recovery and Development, 1986-1990 (UNPAAERD). This document basically reiterated Accelerated Development's key themes by emphasizing agriculture and macroeconomic reforms. Despite the unpopularity of the economic reforms of APPER and UNPAAERD, compliance was said to be high among African governments, but the promised financial contributions from the West failed to follow.

Although it would appear that the battle for control of Africa's development agenda has been won by international development agencies, serious ideological differences continued to impede real progress. The confusion of development agendas became even more pronounced when, in 1989 the World Bank added another endogenous variable responsible for African economic crisis-- governance--and began to require liberalization and democratization for participation in its programs.

The mistrust of the international development agencies' agenda for Africa is described by the OAU Secretary General, Salim Salim, in 1990. "We are told that our crisis is a result of poor administration...We are told to open up government systems and make them accountable to the governed. We are also told to weed out corruption and inefficiency. I agree with all this. But if Africa did all this would development be certain?"

The Bretton Woods Institutions' Response To Sub-Saharan African Crisis In The Early 1980s

As the level of the external debt of most African countries reached unsustainable proportions, the two major BWIs reassessed their roles and proffered remedies which together came to be known as structural adjustment programs (SAPs). The new thinking among IFIs was that a strong correlation exists between political democracy and economic efficiency. As a result, emphasis was placed on "accountability, rule by law and transparency in decision-making."

In order to discourage unwise policies, eligibility for the World Bank's loans were made contingent on a government's acceptance of specified macroeconomic reforms. In other words, the early SAPs were only concerned with governments' commitment to open their economies to global competition and discontinuity of "Import Substitution Industrialization" (ISI), factors believed to inhibit the growth of the private sector. Once agreements were reached, the Bank issued three kinds of loans. Structural Adjustment Loans (SALs) were intended to help a government implement macroeconomic policies. Sector Adjustment Loans (SECALs) were to be used for reforms "at the sectoral level", while "hybrid loans" were given for "investment" and "adjustment" purposes. The IMF later made loan disbursements contingent on what it called the "Structural Adjustment Facility" which was basically designed to ensure the recipients' commitment to free market and efficient production.

Hence, by the late 1980s, the BWIs had linked the political and economic performance of SSA regimes to loan disbursement by demanding "microeconomic reforms," that is, domestic economic reforms and good governance. The World Bank's rationale for this policy shift was as follows: "good governance", that is, greater political accountability, freer press, and transparency of governmental activity would have a "positive effect on economic development" in SSA countries. This policy shift is ironic since in the past, authoritarian regimes were relied upon to implement adjustment programmes. A more plausible explanation for the sudden popularity of political conditionality appears to be the changing international context.

The collapse of the communist regimes of Eastern Europe in 1989 (1991 for USSR) and the consequent proliferation of market-based democracies "revived desire to institutionalize new forms of political accountability in Africa." Furthermore, the opening of the apartheid system had begun in the late 1980s. The dramatic birth of democracy in South Africa in 1994 added a new sense of urgency to the process of economic and political liberalization in the rest of Africa.

Thus, the policy shift within the BWIs at the end of the 1980s should be seen as a response to the international systemic change. It became possible for the BWIs to impose political conditionality when the only viable alternative model, communism, often used as an excuse to support African dictators, was defeated. It is not at all surprising that Western-dominated institutions, freed from systemic constraints, would seek to advance Western democratic system. Whether or not this bodes well for Africa will ultimately depend on the nature of domestic socio-political conflicts in Africa and the extent to which such conflicts are manageable in a liberalized political setting.

Western Donors And Aid Conditionality In SSA

Until 1989, Western donors' responses to the African crises were still largely guided by Cold War imperatives. Todd Moss has pointed out that most observers of U. S. foreign policy now agree that the Cold War imperatives prevented the United States from openly backing liberation fighters in African Portuguese colonies in Africa. The reason: "concern for a strategic North Atlantic Treaty Organization (NATO) base in Azores." It was the fear of the spread of communism in Southern Africa that also compelled the United States to maintain friendship with the Apartheid regime in the 1980s. While the United States' foreign policies were not always congruent with its European allies, it can be safely stated that the latter's foreign policies were not too far off from the former's.

But with the strategic imperatives gone, marked by the collapse of the Soviet empire, good governance also entered the vocabulary of Western donors. In June 1990, President Mitterrand announced at the francophone summit at La Baule that French aid to francophone Africa would henceforth be tied to the establishment of "true democracies with multi-partyism, free elections and respect for human right." The then United States Secretary of State, Warren Christopher, echoed the same sentiment when in May 1993, he promised American economic aid once multi-party elections were held in South Africa.

What could have been the motivation(s) for this belated commitment to building democracy in SSA? Ideology, humanitarianism economics, security, or a combination of two or more of the above. Douglas Brinkley has warned that the United States' call for good governance in SSA should not be taken as an altruistic gesture toward the African people. He further argued that the Clinton doctrine of "democratic enlargement" has been more about America economic competitiveness in the post-Cold War period than promoting "constitutional democracy and human rights everywhere."

The above assertion by Brinkley appears to be confirmed in the Clinton administration's policy in Nigeria, where economic calculations have made democratization and human rights epiphenomena. The annulment of the 1993 election results had been followed by remilitarization and widespread human rights abuses.

Hundreds of opposition activists, human rights campaigners, journalists and trade union officials" are in prison, including the presumed winner of the June 12, 1993 election, Chief M. K. O. Abiola. The United States' response, however, has been cool at best. Carothers has observed that democracy cannot be pushed in Nigeria because the Clinton Administration is "mindful that Nigeria is a major supplier of oil to the United States and that a unilateral U. S. embargo on Nigerian oil would end up benefitting European oil companies and causing little economic harm to Nigeria."

In contrast to the above view, Strobe Talbott posits that idealism and values have historically played a critical role in American involvement in the world and still do today. Others see the United States' democracy promotion as necessitated by security concern. They argue that growing global interdependence and technological advances make the security of Western democracies "bound up with the nature of political order in less established polities."

Do Western donors give aid for humanitarian reasons? Some have rejected the supposition that the West gives aid for altruistic reasons as clearly argued by the following statement: "it is a fallacy to suppose that aid is given grudgingly..., there are strong political interests supporting the aid programme of each country....any reduction in or suspension of aid is deplored by those who depend for their profits or livelihood on its continuation." I argue here that a combination of idealism and realism have motivated the West to give aid.

PART IV

Assessing The Impact Of Conditionality

Have structural adjustment programs been successful? Have economic reforms promoted democratization? I will briefly assess the impact to date of economic liberalization and democratization for African development. There are differing interpretations of the political and economic liberalization in SSA. Differences in perception hinge on two distinct factors. First is the incompatibility of the objectives of the actors involved in the liberalization efforts. Second, reform efforts in SSA are fraught with contradictions and inconsistencies. Both areas will be probed further in this section and the concluding part.

From the perspectives of Africans, the structural adjustment programs have largely failed. They have led to misery for the majority of the SSA population without producing the economic upswing promised. SAPs have ironically been exploited politically to portray the IFIs as the villain, thereby buying time for African dictators. While Africans welcome political reform, they are quick to point out the negative impact of economic reform on the disadvantaged masses. The argument is that if their conditions are not alleviated, discontented citizens will reject democracy. SAPs, to many Africans, are antithetical to the goal of democratization. The social dislocation engendered by SAP, the inflationary effect, scarcity, unemployment and reduced government expenditure have led Nigerians to dub the program "stomach adjustment pain." Here is how Anyang 'Nyongo sums it up:

We are much likely to see democracy survive in economically prosperous countries than in those that are backward and suffering from mass poverty. Economic prosperity necessarily produces the grave diggers for political authoritarians....if nothing is done to increase employment....and if deindustrialization

> continues in the whole of Africa as a result of structural
> adjustment programs, then one might as well kiss democracy
> goodbye beyond the year 2000.

There is an inherent contradiction in the IFIs' conception of democracy as a requisite for development, and that of Africans, as indicated in the above quote, who assume development as a requisite for democracy. These views reflect the on-going debate in the theory of democratic transition. Schmitter and Karl question whether liberal capitalism "necessarily furthers the consolidation of democracy." O'Donnell and Schmitter cast further doubt on the wisdom of a simultaneous pursuit of economic and political liberalization. They argue that obtaining a balance between social democracy and economic democracy during the period of transition can be very crucial in determining whether or not political democracy is consolidated. Perhaps both concepts are mutually reinforcing.

The United Nations Economic Commission for Africa (UNECA) has been critical of the World Bank in SSA. This UN specialized agency utilized the World Bank's own data and report on SALs which showed a 1.8 percent decline in GDP of the SSA countries under SAPs. In addition, the report also shows that after implementation of SAPs, SSA experienced decreased investment levels and higher budget deficits than before. UNECA concluded that poverty level has risen in SSA as a result of SAPs of the 1980s and wrote:

> Underlying the current adjustment programs is the well-known argument, based on classical economic theory, that output, employment, and prices (including wages, interest rates, and exchange rates) are best determined by the free play of market forces, and that prices are the most effective instruments for the efficient allocation of resources. In the African situation (however) the simple truth is that many countries have moved toward free markets without being in a position to take full advantage of available market opportunities because of low capacity to adjust their production structures....These rigidities imply that the main burden of adjustment has been borne by drastic reductions in domestic expenditures with serious economic and social consequences that have tended in many case to retard rather than promote the process of structural transformation.

Another major criticism of SAPs is akin to that of foreign aid in general and is usually echoed by some African economists. To them, aid is simply a lifeblood for authoritarian rulers. The "aid syndrome," they claim, saps, rather than invigorates the economy. With respect to democratization, foreign aid is also said to "erode political will and commitment to reform."

What about those elections in the early 1990s? Judging from the results, conditionality has not had much impact on the SSA political arenas, unless one is willing to strip "democracy" of essential elements noted above. What the world is witnessing is that elections have simply served to legitimize authoritarian leaders in much of the continent.

If Arap Moi of Kenya, Gnassingbe Eyadema of Togo, Henri Konan Bedie of Cote d' Ivoire, Paul Biya of Cameroon and Zimbabwe's Robert Mugabe were as notoriously corrupt as have been depicted and if they shared responsibility for plundering their countries' wealth, then their return to office at the ballot smacks of grand electoral chicanery. In short, these African leaders have demonstrated their political craftiness by neutralizing all potential threats accompanying democracy. Not only have they fooled the international donors and lenders, their survival has mystified civil society in various countries who were left wondering how the African authoritarian leadership could have subverted such an elaborate democratic rescue mission.

African authoritarian leaders have ironically used conditionality to cement their position of power. Elliot Berg points out that the World Bank's official statement that compliance to conditionality in SSA was high in the 1980s was often exaggerated. There was a tacit agreement between African leaders and BWIs officials that compliance was no more than a formality. For instance, a newspaper advertisement for the sale of a state enterprise usually passed for privatization compliance, whether or not privatization actually occurred. The view from Africa is that the Western donors and lenders actually "impede the democratization process by bailing out failed dictators" who continue to wreak havoc on their citizens.

Some observers are quick to point to the defeat of Zambia's Kenneth Kaunda, Malawi's Kamuzu Banda, and Benin's Matthew Kerekou as evidence of a democratic inroad. Actually, a reversal has occurred in Benin and Kerekou has come back. Furthermore, some newly elected presidents have fallen prey to patronage-based politics. They are stifling the very process that helped bring them to power. Since defeating Zambia's long-time dictator, Kenneth Kaunda in 1991, Frederick Chiluba has revealed his own authoritarian side by sacking ministers at will and keeping potential challengers from political competition.

In Uganda, Yoweri Museveni clings to power by insisting that political parties are unnecessary. Ethiopia and Eritrea have provided no democratic opening either. In Ghana, Kenya, Cameroon, Togo and Cote d' Ivoire, incumbent rulers held onto power after elections. In the Nigerian case, the military government of General Sani Abacha simply bought off the pro-democracy community while those who refused to be bought were executed on spurious charges, jailed, or forced into exile. Commenting on what he described as "the containment of the third wave in Africa," Julius Ihonvbere had this to say: "The new political parties and movements have not effectively challenged the autocratic basis and patterns of politics on the continent. True, military regimes are being forced to give up power or to civilianize, as in Ghana, and one-party governments are being compelled to open up, as in Kenya. Yet the autocrats remain effectively in power."

PART V

Democracy, Ethnicity And Class In SSA.

A major distinction between Western and African societies which has so far doomed Western political institutions in SSA is that the latter are characterized by ethnic pluralism and linguistic diversity, while class distinction is more prevalent in the former. Arthur Lewis argues that failure in efforts to introduce effective democracy in Africa was predictable because:

> What is good for a class society is bad for plural society.... The doctrine that the majority shall have its way has become central to the political institutions of class societies... In a plural society this view of politics is not just irrelevant: it is totally immoral, inconsistent with the primary meaning of democracy, and destructive of any prospect of building a nation in which different people might live together in harmony... The democratic problem in a plural society is to create political institutions which give all the various groups the opportunity to participate in decision-making, since only thus can they feel that they are full members of a nation, respected by their more numerous brethren, and owing equal respect to the national bond which holds them together.

The comment by Lewis encapsulates the predicament faced by many SSA states and calls for further elaboration. In contrast to the early periods of nation-building in the United States where economic differences of the three regions - industrial economy in the north, cotton-growing economy in the south, and the westward expansion- were major sources of political conflict, SSA has an added dimension of chronic ethnic conflicts which further complicates its growing pains. In the United States, divergences in regional economic interests mostly threatened the nation's unity as demonstrated in the nullification issues of 1828 and later, the Civil War.

Lewis's point that democracy as practiced in the West would not work in ethnically divided societies has been vindicated. Were American democracy to be imitated in multiethnic states, the spoils system would mean a permanent exclusion of significant ethnic collectivities within those states. Thus, the Ibo and Yoruba groups who together constitute about 47 percent of the Nigerian population, would be perpetually subjugated because of the north's numerical superiority and the winner-take-all democracy.

In short, the industrial revolution transformed Western societies in ways unlikely to be matched in Africa for a long time. In Western societies, social classes, voluntary associations, and ideological differences often determine one's political affiliation. This is not the case in SSA. Individual identity and perception of "significant others" is based on family kinship and ethnicity. Where ethnic collectivities correspond with clearly demarcated territories, as in Nigeria, sectionalism is interpreted by economic as well as ethnic interests. Even among the educated elite, emotional investment in class and interest group politics tends to be tenuous. It is the commitment to one's ethnic group and its interests that is paramount. The stubborn persistence of ethnicity in SSA has rendered the postulations of modernization theories irrelevant in SSA.

PART VI

Conclusions

Admittedly, a full assessment of the current wave of democratization in Africa may be pre-mature. However, by assessing the changes of the past seven years, we can begin to understand why some efforts have succeeded while others have failed. I have attempted in this study to contribute to this cumulative knowledge. I argued that the change in the BWIs policies toward African states resulted from the international systemic change brought on by the demise of communism. The shift in the BWIs policy represents an effort to consummate the triumph of Western political and economic ideologies. Although Africans have struggled for democracy since independence, the current wave of democratization was largely set in motion by systemic factors. Nevertheless, sustaining it, as we have learned, would not be easy. For one thing, external agents' (e.g. Western donors and the BWIs) understanding of "success" is incomplete without attention to such domestic political realities of African states as political activism and ethnicity.

Future research in democratization and development needs to address the unsettled question of the relevance of Western development model in non-Western societies. Furthermore, the perennial question of whether democracy is necessarily a universal truth and aspiration of all peoples remains to be satisfactorily answered. The parameters in this debate have been set by Samuel Huntington and Francis Fukuyama. Huntington's pessimism is unmistakable when he writes: "The end of ideologically defined states in Eastern Europe and the former Soviet Union permits traditional ethnic identities and animosities to come to the fore." He then predicts that the West's promotion of liberal capitalism as a universal value would "engender countering responses from other civilization." Fukuyama, on the other hand, proclaims the end of history. His ideas are akin to the progress theories of the Renaissance and Enlightenment. He interprets the fall of communism to mean "the end of ideological conflict, and with it the end of history," and the beginning of an era in which the spread of Western political and economic ideologies would reign unchallenged everywhere.

The political and economic liberalizations in SSA appear to support both of the above analyses. For example, the actions of of the BWIs and Western donors, in using their financial leverage to encourage liberal values in Africa, support Fukuyama's position. On the other hand, support for Huntington's analysis can be found in resistance to liberal democratic values emanating not only from longtime dictators, but also from the new breed of leaders presumed to be democratically minded. We now know that many of these new leaders are democratic only until inaugurated as leaders of their countries.

Theories of democratic transition and consolidation generally seek to account for two things: first, what are the factors (endogenous and exogenous) responsible for reform initiation and eventual transition from authoritarianism to democracy. The second area of concern to democratization theorists is institutionalization or consolidation of democracy. The problem is that many of these theories have failed to address the issue of development and/or political economy and how it might affect democratization in SSA. Furthermore, most pioneer studies have focused on Europe and Latin America. They are case studies from which generalizations can only be made at some peril. In a sense, current theories of democratization share the problem of universal solutions with the early theories of political development discussed above.

One lesson that SSA can learn from Southern Europe and Latin America is military disengagement from politics. But here, too, international support has not been forthcoming. It is a fact that the United States' imposing presence was instrumental (sometimes decisive) in the process of demilitarization in Latin America in the 1980s and 1990s. Panama, Nicaragua, and Haiti are recent examples. The colonial legacies of Latin America and Africa were quite different. De-ethnicization of Latin

America, evident in the Spanish cultural and religious assimilation, decimation of the indigenous Indian population and mass imposition of Catholicism, largely neutralized ethnically-based politics.

Despite their pronouncements, the objectives of BWIs and Western donors are often contradictory. Also because of their eagerness to lend, BWIs have neglected to hold the SSA regimes to their own borrowing requirements. Another related but different problem is the difficulty of enforcement owing to the conflicting objectives of the Western governments and the IFIs. It would be erroneous to subsume the interests of the Western powers, let alone the BWIs, in SSA. Domestic politics, special interests and even rivalry (e. g. France and the United States in SSA) exert centrifugal forces which continue to make an international efforts at democratization in SSA a disarticulated exercise.

Differences in objectives mean that donors and IFIs have different measures and standards for success. For instance a World Bank report on the SAPs in SSA through 1990 concluded that of the 37 SSA in its program, only Ghana and Tanzania were "successful performers." It is highly unlikely that these two countries would be deemed successful had democratization been a serious conditionality.

An important reason for the diametrically opposed perceptions of political and economic reform in Africa stems from the seemingly divergent objectives of Africans and the international development agencies. On the one hand, international development agencies tend to view democracy as an end in itself. Ordinary people in Africa often see democracy as a means to an end--development. For any successful consolidation in SSA, differences in objectives must first be reconciled. Otherwise, blame for the pains of economic reforms might actually be used by undemocratic rulers to secure their grip on power as they portray outside agents as the culprits. On the other hand, mass disillusionment might provide a rationale for military coups.

The jury is still out on whether Africans failed democracy or democracy failed Africans. If democracy is *sine qua non* for development as touted by the West, then the "Third Wave" has all the trappings of a "false start".

NOTES

*Author's note: Earlier drafts of this work were presented at the Northeastern Political Science Meeting, Philadelphia, PA (November, 1997) and The International Studies Association Meeting, Minneapolis, MN (March, 1998). I am grateful to Christopher Bischoff, professors Sarah Mendelson and Holly Sims of The Graduate School of Public Affairs, University at Albany-SUNY, for their editorial comments and suggestions.

1.I would stress that international policy toward SSA regarding political and economic liberalization is by no means monolithic. Significant differences still exist among Western donors and among various departments within some donor countries. My point is simply that a semblance of coherence in their policies have resonance throughout SSA. For a good analysis of conflicting motivations among Western donors, see Larry Diamond, *Promoting Democracy in The 1990s: Actors and Instruments, Issues and Imperatives*, New York: Carnegie Corporation, 1995, pp. 39-59.

2.Derrick K. Gondwe, *Political Economy, Ideology and the Impact of Economics on the Third World* (New York: Praeger, 1992), p. 94.

3.Ike Udogu, ed., *Democratization in Africa* (Leiden: E.J. Brill, 1997),p.7 4.Larry Diamond et al., *Democracy in Developing Countries: Africa, Vol. Two* (Boulder: Lynne Rienner Publishers, 1988), p. xvi.

5 . Gerald M. Meier, *Leading Issues in Economic Development* 6th ed. (Oxford: Oxford University Press, 1995), p. 7.

6.Ibid.

7. See Ben Turok, ed., *Debt and Democracy,* Vol. 3 (London: Institute for African Alternatives, 1991), pp. 1-10.

8.The terms international development agencies and international development community are used interchangeably to refer to the various agencies involved with development projects in Africa such as the BWIs and other United Nations agencies.

9.Hans Kohn, *Nationalism: Its Meaning and History* (New York: D. Van Nostrand Company, 1965), p. 61.

10.Robert W. July, *A History of the African People* (New York: Charles Scibner's Sons, 1980), p. 368.

11.Ibid., p. 366.

12.Harvey Glickman, *Ethnic Conflict and Democratization in Africa* (Atlanta: The African Studies Association Press, 1995), p. 20.

13.Claude Ake, *Democracy and Development in Africa* (Washington, D.C., The Brookings Institution, 1996), p. 19.

14.Aguibou Y. Yansane, ed., *Development Strategies in Africa* (Westport: Greenwood Press, 1996), pp. 10-11.

15. Ibid., p. 11.

16. Ibid., p. 11

17. Ibid., p. 10..

18. Peter O. Olayiwola, *Petroleum And Structural Change in a Developing Country: The Case of Nigeria* (Westport: Praeger Publishers, 1987), p. 20.

19. See, for instance, Howard J. Wiarda, "Concepts and Models in Comparative Politics" in Dankwart A Rustow and Kenneth Paul Erickson, eds., *Comparative Political Dynamics: Global Research Perspectives* (New York: HarperCollins, 1991).

20.Ibid., p. 33.

21.Ibid., p. 34.

22.Kofi Buenor Hadjor, *Dictionary of Third World Terms* (London: I. B. Tauris & Co. Ltd., 1992), p. 100.

23. Harry Eckstein, Regarding Politics: *Essays on Political Theory, Stability, and Change* (Berkeley: University of California Press, 1992), pp. 232-243.

24. Ibid., p. 242.

25. Ibid.

26. Dankwart A. Rustow and Kenneth Paul Erickson, eds. Comparative Political Dynamics (New York: Harper Collins, 1991), p. 36

27. Ibid., p. 41.

28 There are at least three variants of dependency theories. The earlier version preclude capitalist development in the developing world owing to the exploitative relationship with the advanced capitalist countries. Some dependentistas like Cardoso emphasize the role of "comprador bourgeoisie" in the dependent countries. The World-system variant is more flexible by adding semi-periphery to account for the NICs countries. For more, see Immanuel Wallerstein, *The Capitalist World-Economy* (Cambridge: Cambridge University Press, 1979) and Fernando H. Cardoso and Enzo Faletto, *Dependency and Development in Latin America* (Berkeley, University of California Press, 1979).

29.The role of Western Enlightenment in modernization and political development of Afro-Asian states is discussed extensively in Joseph Rothschild , *Ethnopolitics: A Conceptual Framework* (New York: Columbia University Press, 1981).

30. W. Rand Smith, "International Economy and State Strategies," *Comparative Politics* April (1993), pp. 352-354.

31 .Kjell J. Havnevik, ed. *The IMF And The World Bank in Africa: Conditionality Impact And Alternatives* (Uppsala: Ekblad & Co, Vastervik, 1987), p. 10.

32.This information was provided by Matthew F. Mchugh, a former U. S. Representative and currently an advisor to World Bank President, James Wolfensohn, at a speech delivered at State University of New York, Albany on April 18, 1997.

33. Kjell J. Havnevik, ed. *The IMF And The World Bank in Africa* (Uppsala: Ekblad & Co, Vasterik, 1987), p. 11.

34.Ibid

35 On the marginalization of Africa in the world economy, see for instance, Paul Collier "the Marginalization of Africa," *International Labour Review*, 134, Nos. 4-5 (1995 and Richard Stubbs and Geoffrey R. D. Underhill. eds., *Political Economy and the Changing Global Order* (New York: St. Martin's Press, 1996).

36.This summary is based on an excellent study on the collapse of the Senegalese economy by Catherine Boone, *Merchant Capital and the Roots of State Power in Senegal 1930-1985.* (Cambridge: Cambridge University Press, 1992).

37. An excellent account of this controversy on which much of this section relies is the chapter, "A Confusion of Agendas" in Claude Ake, *Democracy and Development in Africa* (Washington, D. C., The Brookings Institution, 1996).

38. Ibid., p. 24.

39. Ibid
40. Ibid.
41. Ibid., pp. 24-27.
42. Ibid., pp. 28-29.
43. Ben Turok, ed., *Alternative Strategies for Africa: Debt and Democracy* (London: Institute for African Alternatives, 1991), p. 4.
44. Aguibou Y. Yansane, *Development Strategies in Africa* (Westport: Greenwood Press, 1996), P. 31.
45. Ben Turok, ed, *Alternative Strategies For Africa: Debt and Democracy* (London: Institute for African Alternatives, 1991), p. 3.
46. Daniel M. Schydlowsky, ed. *Structural Adjustment: Retrospect and Prospect* (Westport: Praeger, 1995), p. 4.
47. Ibid
48. Ibid.p23
49. Ibid.
50. Douglas Rimmer, ed. *Action in Africa: The Experience of People Actively Involved in Government, Business, Aid* (London: The Royal African Society, 1993), p. 15.
51. Ibid., p. 13.
52. Todd J. Moss "U. S. Policy And Democratization in Africa: The Limits of Liberal Universalism," *Journal of Modern African Studies*, 33, 2 (1995),p. 193
53. Ibid.
54. Douglas Rimmer, ed. *Action in Africa: The Experience of People Actively Involved in Government, Business, Aid* (London: The Royal African Society, 1993), p. 14.
55. Ibid.
56. Douglas Brinkley "Democratic Enlargement: The Clinton Doctrine," *Foreign Affairs*, (Spring 1997), p. 116.
57. Thomas Carothers, "Democracy Without Illusions," *Foreign Affairs*, 76, No. 1 (January/February 1997), p. 98.
58. Freedom House, Freedom in The World: The Annual Survey of Political Rights & Civil Liberties 1995-1996. p. 57.
59. Thomas Carothers, "Democracy Without Illusions," *Foreign Affairs*, (January/February 1997), p. 98.
60. Strobe Talbott, "Democracy and the National Interest," *Foreign Affairs*, 75, No. 6 (November/December 1996), pp. 47-63.
61. Larry Diamond, "Promoting Democracy in the 1990s," A Report to the Carnegie Commission on Preventing Deadly Conflict, December 1995. p. 2.
62. Douglas Rimmer, ed. *Action in Africa* (London: The Royal African Society, 1993), p. 15.
63. See for instance a special issue of *Africa Today*, "Reassessing Democratic Transitions, 1990-1995," 43, 4 (1996)
64. Ibid., p. 361.
65. Daniel M. Schydlowsky, ed. *Structural Adjustment* (Westport: Praeger, 1995), p. 110.

66. Anyang 'Nyongo, "Overview: Africa 2000!" p. 3 cited in Julius O. Ihonvbere, "Where Is the Third Wave? A Critical Evaluation of Africa's Non-Transition to Democracy'" *Africa Today*, 43, 4 (1996) 361.

67. Phillipe C. Schmitter and Terry Karl, "What Democracy Is .. and Is Not," in Larry Diamond and Marc F. Plattner, eds., *The Global Resurgence of Democracy* (Baltimore: Johns Hopkins, 1993), p. 50.

68. Guillermo O'Donnell and Phillipe C. Schmitter, "Tentative Conclusions about Uncertain Democracies," in *Transitions from Authoritarian Rule* p. 12

69. Elliot Berg, "African Adjustment Programs: False Attack and True Dilemmas'" in Daniel M. Schydlowsky, ed., *Structural Adjustment* (Westport: Praeger, 1995), p. 95.

70. UNECA, quoted in ibid., p. 91 .

71 . George B. N. Ayittey "Why Structural Adjustment Failed in Africa," in Daniel M. Schydlowsky, *Structural Adjustment* (Westport: Praeger, 1995), p. 114.

72. Douglas Rimmer, ed. *Action in Africa* (London: The Royal African Society, 1993), p.

73. Elliot Berg "African Adjustment Programs," in Daniel M. Schydlowsky, *Structural Adjustment* (Westport: Praeger, 1995), p. 90.

74. See Julius O. Ihonvbere, "On the Threshold of Another False Start"? in E. Ike Udogu, ed., *Democracy and Democratization in Africa* (Leiden: E.J. Brill, 1997), pp. 125-140.

75. Elliot Berg, "African Adjustment Programs," in Daniel M. Schydlowsky, ed., *Structural Adjustment* (Westport: Praeger, 1995), p. 103.

76. Ibid., p. 114.

77. See *Africa Today*, 43, 4, Oct.-Dec. 1996.

78. Ibid., p. 351.

79. Ibid., p. 353.

80. Ibid., pp. 350-351.

81. W. Arthur Lewis, *Politics in West Africa* (Toronto: Oxford University Press, 1965), p. 66.

82. Andrew Peiser and Michael Serber, eds., *U.S. History and Government* (New York: Amsco school Publications, Inc., 1992), p. 92.

83. Samuel Huntington "The Clash of Civilizations?," *Foreign Affairs*, 72, 3 (Summer, 1993), 29

84. Ibid.

85. Quoted in Gabriel Almond and Bingham Powell, *Comparative Politics* Today (New York: HaperCollins, 1996), p. xii.

86. see Guillermo O'Donnell et al, *Transitions from Authoritarian Rule* (Baltimore: Johns Hopkins, 1986)

87. See Crawford Young, *The Politics of Cultural Pluralism* (Madison: University

of Wisconsin Press, 1976)
88. Douglas Rimmer, ed. *Action in Africa* (London: The Royal African Society, 1993), p. 15

Chapter 3

The Military And The Democratization Process In Africa.

Bamidele A. Ojo

Introduction

The growing trend of transition to democratic governance witnessed recently in Africa seem to have stalled in recent years. One of the reasons for the present predicament has been the endemic involvement of the military in politics which makes a study of democratic transition in Africa incomplete without an examination of the role of the armed forces in the process.

Our main goal is therefore to examine the role of the military in the democratization process in Africa which will involve finding out the direct relationship between military interventions and the democratic process.

The goal will therefore be to examine the importance of the military in the democratization process while focusing on:

- the role the military played in the transition process, to ascertain a successful transfer of power and sustenance of the democratic process.

- the role the military has played in undermining the process of democratic transition.

We will examine the characteristic involvement of the military in politics which seem to have contributed to the present political climate. Secondly, we will examine the nature of the African military which predisposes it to intervening in politics taking cognizance of the fact that the African military is a class in itself which seeks to develop, promote and sustain its interest within the   society. Given its strength as a repository of authorized use of violence, it was able to maintain these interests.

The nature of the State itself becomes central to this study because it creates the condition that allows the military to seek active participation in the political process and therefore allowing the military to undermine any political infrastructure, in an attempt to promoting and sustaining its objectives. By its nature, the African military therefore constitute itself into a power elite, competing for resources and using extra constitutional means(such as violence,bribery, etc.) to attain, retain and maintain power. As opposed to socio-political and economic elites, the military oligarchy remains the most dominant and unhindered participants in the political system, created for and operated by men in uniform. It also restricts(because of its power) the extent   of the involvement of the other participants (political, economic and social elites)in the political process.

What the military has become in Africa, is nothing but a   power conscious oligarchy, who is not only in competition with itself but as a result of its politicization, has lost its reputation and the respect of the people. It has become more corrupt and inept and the temptation to operate as a political group which undermine its aura of infallibility.

However, the military has been able to nurture and create conditions favorable to its retention and maintenance of power by enabling a process that allows it to eliminate those who can challenge its hegemony. In some cases it was able to organize a democratic transformation into an elected leadership, using all the power at its disposal. By doing so, the military guarantees a continual hold on power and preventing the possibility of investigations that might uncover any abuse of power.

The question therefore remains whether the democratic transition is not already compromised. Compromised in the sense that the program itself is a product of minimal or no consultation, created at the mercy of the military and design for its benefit, without an input from the mass of the people. The created structures command no legitimate support from the people. This means that the newly created institutions will have to develop its own legitimacy over a given period of time. Unfortunately, the post military society does not always have the luxury of time, that will allow it to gradually develop and nourish a legitimacy that could sustain such a system. The post military society is endangered from its inception and may within a short period, be interrupted by another set of military opportunists.

The Military in Africa.

The military is used to applying organized violence in defense of the State, mainly in foreign affairs- especially in maintaining the sovereignty and territorial integrity of a State. The State also having the right and duty to employ violence in support of constitutional law and shield itself against external danger uses the military.

The military in its involvement in politics however has abused this legitimate function by encroaching upon political affairs.

The reality is that the military was established to, apply organized violence and by professing to be the guardian of national survival usurp the role and the prerogative in the society which goes beyond democratic legitimacy.

In examining the role of the military and the democratization process in Africa, there is the need to consider the impact of the socio-political and economic environment within which it exists. As a socio-political phenomenon, the military draws its vitality from a complex set of sources within the society - national, social, material and spiritual.   The military by intervening in politics usually in most cases imped democratic process but at the same time displaying a predilection to imposing solutions to that kind of problem [Asbjorn,1980]. Strategically located in the web of state and government bureaucracy and entrusted with the management of the instrument of violence, the military therefore developed a propensity to intervening actively in politics with a view to protecting its own interests rather than those of the Society whom it pledges to serve.

By nature, the military regimes are openly repressive because of their active involvement in the maintenance of internal security and could find allies within the society (both the conservative forces and the working class) who are themselves   eager to seize actions in the State and government largess left vacant as a result of the change in power. In Africa,   the bureaucracy usually play an active role in providing orientation and assisting the new military administrators in the act of governance and by so doing gain tremendous recognition and power but eventually will be politicized as a result of it.

The politicization of the civil service undermines its effectiveness in a post military and democratic government, which needed an impartial, politically neutral and fair-minded bureaucracy. The bureaucracy therefore becomes the source of transmitting clientelist relationship from the previous military administration to the new democratic government, thereby affirming the saying " plus ca change, plus c'est la meme chose".

Military intervention in politics is therefore a direct response to the weakness of socio-economic and political institutions in many of these African states allowing the military to seize power at moments of political stress and crisis[African States do have an abundance of these]. Violence therefore acquires a central importance in the interaction between the military and the public as it administers the country.

Considering the nature of state in Africa (Crawford Young, 1994, Zartman, I.W.(ed), 1995), the problem today is by far more complex and cannot be readily waved off by a mere suggestion and the use of force by the military. In fact it has been the major problem facing the military today as it attempts to force solutions and impose decrees, which is by its nature is normal and as it becomes more autocratic and sometimes totalitarian and kleptomaniacs , it increases anti military sentiment among the population.

The inability to resolve the socio-political and economic malaise becomes too difficult for the military to accept and represent a failure which runs contrary to their strict military ethics. In politics you concede defeat but in the military, you cannot concede defeat. The contradiction resulting thereof, is difficult to deal with and uncommon to the military thinking which is not independently shaped but whose ultimate solution predicates on the use of force.

The military mind and attitude is conditioned by long socialization process affected through professional training and indoctrination becomes one of its main obstacles when it intervene in politics and the first to suffer from the involvement and therefore dooming the regime.

The attitude formed by the military, authoritarian by nature and given the diverse political environment in many African states, generate in many instances, ethnocentric and coercive actions as a means to achieving its goals.

One of the characteristics of the State in Africa, are its weakness and its decaying nature (Zartman,I.W.,(ed),1995), which predispose it to absence of legitimacy and a lack of respect for authority, thereby making it a fertile ground for economic and socio-political chaos. And it is in response to this "etat d'affaires" that the military justify the initial takeover by acting as if it is the only remedy to the situation by claiming to have the organizational effectiveness, the discipline and the desire to enhance national sovereignty and security.

The military profess the ability to promote national integration and nation-building against the threat of ethnic fragmentation. But in the past thirty years, the contrary has been the case. It has however demonstrated its capacity to advance social mobility and at promoting the interest of the middle class, to which some of the officers themselves belong.

The Democratization Process.

The military present itself as an agent of democracy which in itself is ironic because, it has violated constitutional provisions before taking over power and therefore turning around by promising democracy, does not in any way make them an agent of democracy. But it is a reality that in many African States, it is the military who has had to guarantee and manage transitional programs.

Whatever the origin of the new political design, it is usually expected to guarantee fundamental human rights, the rule of law, multiparty politics, periodic elections and free market economy, among others. Democracy will provide the people the opportunity to participate in the political process while guaranteeing a more responsible and accountable government(Ojo, B.1998,1997, 1993 & 1994).

However, each society because of its own unique experience should develop its own democratic process and modalities. Democracy does not exist in a vacuum. It exists within a cultural milieu. It is therefore quite counterproductive for democratic "engineers" in Africa to ignore the socio-cultural environment within which their new experiments will operate. The attempt to replicate American, British or French systems in any Africa society could therefore be a journey in futility.

The total adaptation of these foreign democratic experiments like in all other institutions in many African states today, involve even the minutest of details.

For example, asking candidates to pay exorbitant registration fees in order to be able to run for political office. In Nigeria, in the canceled Presidential election of June 12, 1993, prospective candidates were asked to pay between N100,000 and 500,000 (Naira) and in South Africa(the April 27, 1994 election) the registration fee was $21,000, when the majority of the population cannot afford a tenth of that amount and while most of them live in poverty.

Domestic variables were also ignored in the transition process. Among them are the roles of the traditional African institutions such as the traditional rulers. These institutions were not absorbed into new political structures. Whereas these institutions probably hold the key to legitimate sources of authority that could provide the foundation for democratization on the continent.

The recent drive toward democracy has however been stalled by simultaneous activities on the other end of the spectrum [Stephen Riley, 1993]. For example, the much heralded democratic changes are either still a dream in Nigeria, Kenya or non existent in Zaire today.
Sierra Leone is under military rule. Autocratic leadership continues in Togo, Cameroon, Uganda and Malawi, to mention a few. Political changes are yet to be consolidated and democratic regimes are yet to be legitimized. Democratic pressures are having uneven impact because political leaders continue to resist or deflect the demand of pro-democratic groups.

Many of these leaders engineered these changes, manipulated and at the same time obstruct the process for their own political gain. Before being forced out by Kabila, Mobutu Sese Seko for example, divided domestic pro-democratic opposition in order to continue to hold on to. In Nigeria, Babangida declared the election of June 1993 null and void and thus denied Chief M.K.O. Abiola the possibility of assuming the presidency of the Third Republic. Abiola, although died on the eve of his release from prison, by Abacha's successor (after the military tyrant died suddenly on June 8, 1998),on July 7,1998 could be credited for possibly laying the foundation for pragmatic politics in Nigeria

Babangida later resigned and installed a transitional government headed by a civilian[technocrat], Chief Sonekan, from the same State and ethnic group as Chief Abiola. The transitional government failed in its attempt to continue the transition program and was eventually forced out of power by its defense chief and the former deputy to Babangida, Sani Abacha, at the same time suspending all existing democratic institutions already initiated as part of the transition program. He also set in motion another transition program of its own that has been changed several time but now due to establish an elected government by the year 1998.In Kenya, Arap Moi continues to hold on to power while suppressing pro-democracy movements.

In Zambia however, Kaunda was defeated at the polls and he willingly accepted the will of the people while Rawlings [in Ghana] became a civilian President and won an election more or less in Egyptian tradition. There have been changes also in Benin, Togo and Equatorial Guinea. In 1989 for example, 35 countries were governed under a single party system and all except Malawi has adopted multiparty competition providing choice and more participation for their people. There are changes also in Congo, Mali and Sao Tome & Principe. In all these countries[Equatorial Guinea, Togo and Zaire among others], pro- democracy movement and oppositions forced autocrats to accept the inevitable- a need for democratization. However, human rights abuses continue in many of them and Instability and civil strife characterizes others(like Somalia, Ethiopia,Liberia Rwanda and Burundi).

These are examples of the weakness and political decay experienced in many African states and the inability to maintain national unity, especially in the face of diverse ethnic composition compounded by an overlay and overlap of historic Kingdoms [a colonial legacy]. In fact, one of the justifications for limiting popular self-determination was and is still is, inter ethnic conflict resulting from multiethnic composition of many African states.

Praetorian Tendency:

The military intervention in politics in Africa is not a fluke but an organized and deliberate attempt at political survival and social mobility. Considering the fact that the military has been subjected to intense politicization during the period of colonization and immediate post independence period, they developed a predisposition toward governance as a means of promoting their (group) interest.

Its origin could be traced to the colonial use of brute force, when it(military) became an appropriate tool for the exploitation of Africans and the suppression of all opposition.

At independence, the military played the same role in sustaining power for the post independent leadership and in maintaining political order, in otherwise chaotic societies. The result of which led to the civil and military spheres becoming congruent and a tendency for the military sphere to spread into the civil sphere of the society. The politicization gave the military an insight into political governance while realizing that it not only sustains civilian governments but could control power for itself.

The military, concealed behind its "core" values and "sense of ethics"[viz. order, discipline, hierarchy, obedience and devotion to the interest of the fatherland] present itself as a protector of the working class and disguised it as its concern for the general interest of the community.

Within the military itself there is also the self-conscious, self-righteous belief in the superiority of the military bureaucratic organization over democratic institutions and activities of the politicians. While the State crisis of the 1960s created the need to transfer responsibility for planning, security and some state functions to the armed forces, as the least poorly functioning branch of the government, the increased revenues accrued to the new States especially from crude oil, etc. , enabled the governments to direct additional funds toward the purchase of arms and military hardware, indirectly increasing the wealth and capability of the military. The unexpected modernization of the army coupled with increased social roles turned the military organization into a class institution per excellence 'imbued with the political values of the ruling class"[Kuc^uk, 1993].

Although, it does not always operate in the name of these values, it usually presents itself as a non- ideological political force, called upon to guarantee public order and national security. Its assumed role is a function of its perceived socio-political status in the political system- 'Ordained' with the mission to defend the constitutional order[-which in this case represent that of a particular class system], which is represented as patriotic and an affection for the national community. Its intervention is not only seen as patriotic but independent within which its social role coincides with its particular interest. But the helplessness and disaffection of the population with the armed forces increases as the military continue to stay on in power.

The military as a result of its involvement in politics suffers from intra- organizational schism, resulting from competition among and within ranks, which runs contrary to its established code of ethics.

This is because in the political arena, the military find itself dominated by a small group- an elite of the oligarchy, thereby alienating members of the lower class or echelon from the benefits that comes with real political power. For example, only the chosen are trained in the best military schools abroad[- another legacy of colonialism]. The promotion and command positions are therefore based on the contact that you have with the ruling junta. It is no longer based on military ethics and merits. What developed was a neo-patrimonial and clientelist relationship between the rank and file of the military, thereby creating the condition for coups and counter coups.

The military organization also operates within the political process in accordance with its own specific undemocratic values, regardless of the class origin of its officers' corps. As Janowitz rightly put it, "the social background[of officers] emerges as progressively less important than professional experiences and personal alliances in fashioning the outlook of the Military elite"[Janowitz,1971].

The military in the last three decades have turned itself into an important political force and in most cases, the only political force. Its domination is undisputable and cannot be challenged by any other social forces in many of these countries because, the military does have the ability to attract many of its detractors into joining it in governance, thereby frustrating many of its opponents. The military is well organized and equipped to hold on to power, especially because of its use of violence and the use of the largess of the state. It assures social mobility and sustains status of its members and those close to it, in the society. It is even more powerful, if we consider the fact that many of the economic sectors in Africa are state controlled making participation in government a means to accumulating wealth because it is the most viable way for the accumulation of capital.

The problem with the military handling of the democratic transition, is that the process is handled with an eye on sustaining the military interest within the created "democratic structure". The trend is to allow the military not only to handle transition but to be the object of the program, whereby, it seeks election as a democratically elected government, as we saw in Ghana and the attempts now being made in Nigeria. In cases where the military is not involved in a civilianizing process , the ground is laid for possible coup d'etat within a limited period of time, whereby the cycle of transitional programs can be revisited.

This cycles ultimately lead to a praetrorian gap- a cycle of unending military rule. And Nigeria has been experiencing this syndrome since the coup of 1966 but well demonstrated by the transition program of Murtala-Obasanjo that paved the way for a few years of democratic governance under President Shagari in 1979-83, followed by the governments of Buhari-Idiagbon Babangida and Abacha in that order (all military administration)(Ojo,B, 1998).

An End To A Legacy ?

Post independence politics in Africa has been characterized in many instances, by the substitution of army dictatorship for civil rule. More than 70 coups d'etat[successful or abortive] were staged between 1952, when Colonel Nasser of Egypt staged the revolt that overthrew the government of King Farouk, and the bloodless coup of 1968 in Mali. For example, Dahomey(now Benin) and Zaire(with Mobutu ascending to power) experienced series of military activities then.
Army revolts in 1965 deposed Ahmed Ben Bella in Algeria. And in 1966, Burundi and Central African Republic had their civilian administrations replaced by military regimes. Togo and Ghana also witnessed series of coup d'etat between 1960 and 1980 as it was the case in Nigeria, Sierra

leone, Libya, Burkina Faso(formerly Upper Volta), Rwanda and Somalia. Niger, Chad, Liberia and Ethiopia were not left out of this same syndrome. Many of these military interventions had the backing of major powers like France, the United States and Great Britain.

As already indicated, the military has paid for its involvement in politics. The instability and tensions in post independent African States has not only undermine the fabrics of the African military, but its politicization has led to competition within the corps resulting in personnel rivalries and inter ethnic jealousies.

The Military is not a detached and discipline political establishment capable of standing aloof from the forces that surrounds it. It has become as corrupt and inept as its civilian counterpart but its possession of the means of violence allows it to constantly wrestle political control from civilians because it(military) is incapable of doing so under an organized democratic process.

It(the military) lacks the necessary academic ability and usually made up of drop outs and recruits who are incapable of surviving in an electoral and competitive socio- political environment. Under rated by the civil society, it is incapable of holding on to people's trust or gain legitimacy because in most cases it has never fought in a war(although some have little experiences in UN Peace-keeping operations). Taking control of the State apparatus of power was therefore a means toward achieving self- actualization and to forcing the civil society to respect and appreciate it.

In spite of all these, the potential for democratic change on the continent is dependent on the resignation of the military to performing its primary duty- that of maintaining the defense and security of the State. Moreover, if this euphoria for democracy is equated with political pluralism, the tremendous changes that we have been witnessing might induce other African states in the right direction. Given the African political climate these changes are not guaranteed, it could be thwarted by autocrats and the military. For example in Burundi, when the military took over power, it assassinates Melchoir Ndadaye, whose party- The Front for Democracy in Burundi(Frodebu) has just won an election with more than 71%. This intervention torched off civil strife between the Tutsi, the Hutus and other ethnic groups.

In Nigeria, Mashood Abiola, who won the last Presidential election before it was annulled was imprison until his death on July 7, 1998. And in Sierra Leone, young military officers in their mid- 20s, led by Captain Valentine Strasser assumed political power by accident because the military saw itself as a viable option to democratic governance.

The growing acceptance of multiparty politics and 'democracy' as an inevitable outcome, could be attributed to:

The growing resentment against the military regimes and the growth of pro-democracy groups. As popular support dwindles, organized pro-democracy movement arose to the dislike of the military and as it cracks down on opposition, it loses more support.

When Sanni Abacha in Nigeria took over power in 1993, he appointed a junior Brigadier- General to head the Army, which seem to signal an acknowledgment of the restiveness of the middle echelon officers who were openly critical of the continuation in government of the military establishment, overweighted with top level General. The Army headed by this junior Brigadier has within it more than twenty Lt. General and Major- Generals. This scenario runs contrary to military ethics and organizational structure.

The economic difficulties, represented by high rates of inflation and indebtedness seem to be tempting some African military(i.e., Benin), to return to the barracks and to allow civilian politician to assume responsibilities for the implementation of inevitable harsh austerity program(we may probably see them again, when anti civilian administration sentiment increases as a result of the austerity measures).

External powers have also played an important role in the sustenance of military dictators, through military and economic aids and in some cases indirect intervention (In 1964, attempt to restore constitutional rule in Gabon was thwarted by French paratroopers, and there was also, the support the United States offered Mobutu in Zaire).

The new World Order has led to a reevaluation of major power's foreign policy options on the continent. The United States under President Clinton now emphasize that' democracies not dictatorship offers the best means to defend human Rights'. The former United States Secretary of State, Warren Christopher once said that' the people of Africa know where their future lies, not with corrupt dictators like Mobutu(of Zaire) but with courageous democrats in every part of the continent"[West Africa, 12/30-6/ 1993].The British and French supported the same positions and reaffirmed the need to attach any form of aids to the institution of democracy.

Conclusions.

One is tempted to ask whether the transition to democracy is sustainable in Africa, Whether domestic social forces and external pressures are capable of effectively sustaining these changes. Whatever the challenges, these new governments will face, the military will remain an important force in African politics unless, necessary political and economic changes are sustained to change the perception that involvement in politics, provide an avenue for social mobility in the society. Politics should not be seen as a source of getting rich as it is today.

But that can only be possible if there is sustained democratic governance long enough to instill some sense of responsibility on both the governor and the governed. Ironically, the military however remains the guarantor of democratic transition, even after stepping asides, it must develop the courage to resist the temptation to take over in the future. The changes going on around the world are positively impacting on the continent whether it comes from the world bank, the IMF or any of the major power, especially if it relates to the implementation of democratic reform which can be of tremendous importance especially if there is demand for pluralism, public accountability and the respect for the rule of law and human rights as a condition for continuing interaction.

It is important that African States develop independent institutions that will guarantee the transition to democracy and sustain it. There is a need for an impartial civil service, judiciary, military and a stable government devoid of patronage as a step in the right direction. Under colonialism, political institutions were traditionally autocratic and the process of decolonization did not create a deep rooted democratic political institution either. What we had in immediate post colonial Africa, is nothing short of a gestation process, for democratic governance, the failure of democracy to take hold, is an inability to develop domestic variables that could sustain the process.There is also the need to establish a civil- political supervision of the military organization so that it can develop into a professional non- political force. [Huntington, 1957]. It needs to be transformed into a modern institution with specific and constructive role in the society.

Democratic change can also be sustained by increasing the strength and stability of political institution through political consensus [Firer, 1962]. The process should involve national identification and popular participation. The recognition of these ideals will pave the way to socio-political stability that will precipitate socio-political and economic development on the continent.

Democracy is not just a form of government. It is a pattern of thought and a way of life. It presupposes self-discipline and political tolerance, without which it cannot survive. Popular participation is an indispensable part of a democratic framework .And the constitution should be beyond all in the polity because anybody who seeks to overthrow constitutional state should be considered as violating the sacred law of the land and should be treated as such. The Military should not be at liberty to overthrow democratically elected officials whatever the circumstances and the people should be able to demand a respect of its will by whoever lives within the polity. There is the need to institute adequate measures to prevent future military intervention as a guarantee to sustaining democratic governance.

Notes:

1. *Africa Report*(Washington. DC)1993-1994.
2. Asbjorn Eibe & Marek Thee.(1980)*Problems of Contemporary Military.*(New York: St. Martin Press).
3. Andreski.S.(1968),*Military Organization and Society.*(Berkeley: University of California Press).
4. Ejub Kacuk (1980),*The Socio-class determinant of Militarism.*in Asbjorn and Thee,op.cit.
5. Finer S.E.(1962), *The Man Horseback.*(NY: Praeger)p.24-38.
6. Huntington S.P.(1957), *The Soldier and The State.* (Cambridge, Mass: Harvard U. Press).
7. July Robert (1993), *A History of African People*(Prospect Height, illinois: Waveland Press.)
8. Janowitz M.(1971) *The Professional soldier* (New York: The Free Press.)
9]. Ojo Bamidele A.(1998)*(ed)The Nigeria's Third Republic: The Prospects and Problems of Transition to Civil Rule*(Commark, NY: Nova Publish.)
        (1997) *Human Rights in a New World Order: Universality, Acceptability and Human Diversity* (Commark, NY:Nova Publ.)
        (*1993)Peter Pan Sydrome: Africa in World Affairs.* in Muyumba F & Atcherson E. *Pan Africanism :A Cross -cultural Reader* (Needham Height:MA:Ginn Press).
        (1994) "Contending Issues in African Studies: A view from Below" *Wahenga* (Queens University journal of Black History, Fall   1994)
10. Riley Stephen (1993) Africa's new Wind of Change' in *World Politics, Annual Edition. 1993/94*(Guilford,CT: Dushkin Publ.)
11.   Crawford Young (1994),*The African Colonial State In Comparative Perspective* (New Haven,CT: Yale University Press)
12. Study Group on Militarization of the International,/Peace Research Association ,(1978) *Bulletin of Peace Proposal* .NO.2 p.170-178.
13. *West Africa* (London) 1992- 1994.
14. Zartman, I.W,(1995) *Collapsed States: The Distintegration and Restoration of Legitimate Authority.* (Boulder,CO: Lynne Rienner)

Chapter 4

Africa, Economic Recovery And Political Transition

Julius Ihonvbere

Many countries continue to operate in a crisis mode. Many have suffered a deterioration in their international terms of trade. Many are still obliged to pay onerous amounts of foreign exchange in debt service. Some have suffered severe declines in living standards. In short: Africa has yet to break its developmental gridlock.
The Global Coalition for Africa[1].

... the overall performance of the African Economy since 1986 has been dismal. The reasons can be attributed mainly to the debt burden, the collapse of commodity prices, the low-levels of resource-flows from the developed countries, as well as natural calamities .... Africa's debt is crippling. The realities are as startling as they are depressing.
General Ibrahim Babangida[2].

Time and time gain, all across Africa, hopeful steps towards development have stopped because of instability. This cycle can be broken only through the growth of democratic practices ... Today, economic progress requires access to information, right of expression and the necessity for popular participation.
Boutros-Ghali.[3]

This is not necessarily another essay in "afro-pessimism." Even if the purpose is not to pretend as to the serious dimensions and implications of Africa's increasing marginalization and crisis, it seeks to present this crisis as is, and critique some of the current superstructural and superficial responses to the region's predicaments. As well, it hopes to go beyond the current tendency to ignore the substructural or domestic dimensions of the African crisis and pay due attention to developments within civil society and other domestic constituencies in Africa. As the international response to the Somali crisis clearly showed, African states and the Organization of African Unity(OAU) are completely incapable of responding to the region's deepening crisis. The little they have achieved so far, and the region's increasing marginalization in the emerging international division of labor attest to the structural weaknesses of African economies and the nonexistence of viable structures and processes of crisis management and crisis containment.[4]

The position of Ibrahim Babangida cited in the opening quote shows the dangers of "externalizing" the origins and nature of the African crisis. Such an approach undermines domestic potentialities, justifies and rationalizes elite deficiencies and shortcomings, and strengthens the chains of unequal exchange and dependence on the outside world.[5] Three decades and more of reliance on externally-determined ideologies, models of development, and subservience to the powers of the East and West left Africa at the beginning of the 1990s as the most debt distressed, most crisis-ridden, most underdeveloped, most dependent, and most marginal region in the international division of labor. This is not to overlook the role which imperialism, transnational corporations, unequal exchange, and foreign domination and exploitation has played in the generation, consolidation, and reproduction of the African predicament[6].

On the contrary, our position is that persistent complaints about the role of external factors, lead almost no where. Rather, the challenge of global disinterest in Africa, complaints about "aid fatigue," "compassion fatigue" and so on, is to devise credible, viable, and relevant alternatives to previous prescriptions in order to redefine Africa's relations with the outside world and invariably,
the location and role of the region in the global power and economic system. How long will African leaders continue to produce new documents, agreements, charters and declarations? How long will they continue, like Babangida (see above) to complain about external causes of Africa's deepening crisis? How long will they continue to rely on foreign responses and interventions to take care of intra-African problems and crisis as was the case in Somalia? How long will they continue, at varying levels, to rely on foreign military support, foreign aid, and foreign-dictated

models of development and recovery before they design workable programs to contain the deepening crisis of the region? The point is that in so far as Africa remains what it is- underdeveloped, dependent, vulnerable, foreign dominated, unproductive, crisis-ridden and marginal in the global system, neither investors nor donors will take the region seriously.

To be sure, there is no way we can understand the African crisis in a holistic manner without acknowledging the place of its historical experiences and the consequences of that experience. The periods of informal empire, slavery, colonialism, and the programmed transition to neocolonialism, left Africa with distorted and disarticulated institutions and structures. It wiped out extraordinary possibilities, implanted alien tastes, institutions, values, and contradictions. It left Africa with a bifurcated economy, a non-hegemonic and weak state, a weak, dependent and unproductive elite, foreign domination of the economy, concentration on the production and exportation of a
narrow range of cash crops, dependence on foreign technology, skills, goods and services; internal antagonisms based on region, religion, and ethnicity; and marginalization in the global capitalist system into which the region had been structurally incorporated. But we already know all these.

There have been scores of responses to these realities since the 1960s from African socialism, through indigenization and nationalization, to joint ventures and other forms of partnerships with foreign capital. In any case, Africa was not the only region that was colonized, and while the masses of the people have been ready to confront the realities of underdevelopment and dependence, the elites have employed strategies of propaganda, defensive radicalism, political posturing, diversions, and manipulation to reproduce the unequal and exploitative relations with foreign capital to the detriment of their economies and peoples. In the 1960s and 1970s, it was convenient to focus on foreign causes of Africa's problems. Today, it is becoming clear that Africans must look inward for new national orders and struggle to recompose and restructure the domestic political, economic, and social theaters in order to make progress.

In a world system which is increasingly emphasizing domestic policies and regional trade blocs, Africa must face the challenges of the 1990s from a position different from those adopted in the past three decades. In the rest of this chapter we first, examine the depth of the African crisis and its implications for development; second, we examine some responses to the crisis and why they have failed; and third, we propose a holistic alternative to current realities. We would like to point out that constraints of space, will militate against our ability to discuss these issues in detail, though in all instances they will be sufficiently outlined.

The African Predicament: Dependency, Poverty And Maginalization

We have already noted the historical origins of the African crisis. There is no doubting the fact that the colonial experience, more than anything, is responsible for the structured incorporation into, and marginalization of Africa in the global division of labor. However, since political independence in the 1960s, a combination of internal and external developments have contributed significantly to negating possibilities for growth, development, and peace. At the external level, declining foreign investment, rising cost of energy, declining commodity prices, reduced foreign aid, poorly conceived development models, high interest rates and rising prices of imports, and increasing expenditure of arms and defense have drained resources and led to waste and liquidity problems.

As well, the failure of investors to develop local skills, transfer technology, use local raw materials and reinvest surpluses, the demands of debt-servicing, the imposition of tariff and non-tariff barriers on African exports, interference in African affairs, and the manipulation of leaders and domestic policies have also worsened the already bad conditions of Africa. These externally-determined policies were possible only because of the weak and non-hegemonic structure of the African state, bureaucratic inefficiency, and the vulnerability and fragility of African economies. At the domestic levels, African elites and leaders have given a very terrible account of themselves. Most of them have found it rather convenient to blame external actors for their problems while continuing domestic policies that directly challenge and negate possibilities for development.

The suffocation of civil society, massive human rights abuses, waste and mismanagement, unpardonable corruption, political irresponsibility, lack of political will and courage to initiate and implement far-reaching policies, the manipulation of primordial loyalties and differences, and lack of accountability to the people have squandered resources, alienated the people, and reproduced Africa's marginal role in the global economy. As well, the concentration of resources on selected urban locations, the inability to diversify the export base or promote industrialization, massive expenditures on the military, coups and counter-coups, political intolerance, and violence have undermined development plans, scared off investors, and squandered opportunities for growth. Furthermore, the privatization of the state and its resources, misplaced priorities, dependence on foreign tastes, aid, and advice, and total disrespect for indigenous cultures, values and traditions by the new elites have only deepened Africa's vulnerability to foreign penetration, domination, and exploitation.

A catalogue of the region's predicament today is rather frightening. The ECA has declared the 1980s as "Africa's lost Decade."[7] The World Bank argues that Africans are significantly worse of f today than they were at the point of freedom from colonial domination, thirty years ago[8]. The OAU admits that African states have done so badly, they are unable to show any indicator of progress in the past two decades.[9] Edward Jaycox, Vice-President, Africa Region for the World Bank *summarized* the African situation after the second 1979 oil shock thus:

> The region had no industrial base to speak of, its human resource and management skills were extremely thin, its infrastructure was sparse and often run down, its technological options were limited, and it was rapidly losing its competitiveness to other developing regions. Wrong-headed policies fed into and exacerbated these basic problems. Grossly overvalued exchange rates, excessive taxation of exports, widespread price controls and subsidies, state interference in internal and external trade, and generally poor management of the revenues from the commodity price booms of the 1970s all these left Africa in the early 1980s with a major development crisis on is hands.[10]

Since the early 1980s, the situation has rapidly deteriorated on all fronts in Africa. The foreign debt reached $290 billion in 1992 or 90 per cent of Africa's GNP (112 per cent for sub-Saharan Africa). The region became the most debt-distressed region in the world not because of the size of its debt but because of the very high debt-GNP ratio. Debt-servicing began to drain massive resources from the region. For instance, it paid out $26 billion in debt-servicing in 1991 alone. Credit lines were closed as many countries could no longer pay for imports and foreign reserves were severely depleted. Expenditures on health and social services declined by 26 per cent and higher in many instances.

Educational institutions deteriorated to unprecedented levels as once reputable academic establishments became glorified shadows of what they once represented. Crime, violence, riots, prostitution, and social atavism increased as it became more and more difficult for rural and urban people to survive. Governments could not pay wages and salaries and the bureaucracies simply deteriorated further. Corruption in countries like Nigeria, Zaire, and Kenya got out of hand and the delegitimization of the state, its institutions and agents proceeded very rapidly to new levels. According to Boubakar Diaby-Ouattara, Executive Director of The Global Coalition for Africa,

> Throughout Sub-Saharan Africa, agricultural production continued to stagnate, except in a handful of countries .... Soil degradation and deforestation combined with high population growth, portend recurring agricultural crisis ... Unless action is quick and forceful, adverse trends in socioeconomic development may well persist beyond the 1990s, causing untold human suffering and endangering the much desired pluralism and democracy...[11]

Ouattaras fear are informed by the frightening realities in contemporary Africa: of the 38 least developed countries in the world, 28 are in Africa, only 26 per cent of people in sub-Saharan Africa have access to safe drinking water, over 1,000 children are dying daily from avoidable diseases, there are 11 active wars going on in the region, hundreds of thousands have died in war, the region produces half of the world's refugees, unemployment has experienced a fourfold increase since 1970, more than half of the population have no access to heath facilities; and in countries like Liberia, Somalia, and the Sudan, the state can no longer govern.

In addition, food production is 20 per cent lower than 1970 levels and severe malnutrition and food shortages are widespread; there is only one doctor for every 28,000 Africans; and it has the highest population growth rate in the world of 3.2 per cent. It is estimated that 4.8 per cent of GDP is allocated to defense in sub-Saharan Africa. This is the highest in the developing world as the figures for Latin America and South Asia are 1.6 per cent and 3.6 per cent respectively. An estimated $15 billion worth of military equipment and arms were sold to Africa between 1985 and 1989.

The Global Coalition for Africa has reported that "Sub-Saharan Africa's terms of trade with the rest of the world deteriorated throughout the 1980s ... The average index for the region fell almost 23% in 1987. There was scarcely any change until a further fall of 8.9% in 1991"[12] Even the region's capacity to import fell by 14 per cent between 1985 and 1991, net resource transfers to the region declined from $12.7 billion in 1989 to $12.3 billion in 1990 and to $11.7 billion in 1991.[13] Michael Chege has noted that the British alone withdrew 31 per cent of their investment in Sub-Saharan Africa between 1979 and 1989 while private investment declined from a peak of $2.3 billion in 1982 to $900 million in 1989.[14] In short, the catalogue of woes is endless: drought, hunger, wars, disease, frustrations, political cynicism, infrastructural decay, political tensions, bureaucratic inertia, human rights abuses and the asphyxiation of civil society have become commonplace all over Africa. As the ECA notes, the current crisis

> ... is not only an economic crisis but also a human, legal, political and social crisis. It is a crisis of unprecedented and unacceptable proportions manifested not only in the abysmal declines in economic indicators and trends, but more tragically and glaringly in the suffering, hardship and impoverishment of the vast majority of African people.[15]

It was to the deteriorating conditions above and to the failure of national responses to stem the tide of decay and disintegration that the International Monetary Fund(IMF) and World Bank were to respond in the 1980s with monetarist stabilization and structural adjustment programs.[16] Unfortunately, because these policies ignored the political contexts of the African crisis; and because they overlooked the character and quality of leadership, the power of the opposition to resist, the nature of contending constituencies, the depth of the economic crisis, the implications of a highly delegitimized state implementing harsh monetarist policies, and the nature of national political and ideological discourses, stabilization and adjustment policies failed to assist the recovery process in Africa. Indeed, policies and programs of desubsidization, deregulation of prices of goods and services, commercialization and privatization, devaluation, tight fiscal controls, and a floating interest rate increased alienation, political violence and conflicts, coups and counter-coups, inflation, hunger, capital flight, de-industrialization, and serious economic and social dislocation.[17]

The ECA noted in 1990 that orthodox adjustment and stabilization policies "undermine the human condition and disregard the potential and role of popular participation in self-sustaining development".[18] At the 1991 review of the United Nations Program of Action for African Economic Recovery and Development(UNPAAERD), the OAU was clear on the fact that "African economies did not witness any significant change for the better.... from all economic indicators, the continent of Africa appeared to have been by-passed by (the) positive developments in the world system".[19] It is in this context that we can appreciate the rather sober summary of Layashi Yaker, the Executive Secretary of the ECA when he noted that:

... Africa ended the 1980s with more misery and underdevelopment than it started with. Africa was the only continent where all the critical indicators of development showed unacceptable retrogression, and where all the socio-economic and political ills that were so overwhelmingly glaring in the 1980s, and which are still very much around us today in the form of vulnerability to natural disasters, persistent threat of hunger- which now looms over 20-30 million Africans- refugee problems, cycles of drought and environmental degradation, declining productivity and incomes, daunting external debt problems and paucity of external resource flows, worsening terms of trade, persistence of civil wars and the spread of internal strife, etc.[20]

It is obvious therefore, that by the beginning of the 1990s, Africa was already in serious trouble.

Responses To The African Crisis

Domestic and global responses to the African crisis since the 1960s have had almost no positive effect. How else can we explain the horrible conditions highlighted above? Today, there is not one African country that can be described as a Newly Industrializing Country (NIC) talk less being described as a *developed* country, no matter how we stretch the definition of development.

Policies of Africanization or indigenization, nationalization, import substitution, trickle down models or growth pole models of development planning, partnerships with foreign capital, state capitalism through massive state intervention, dependence on foreign aid, and African socialism to name a few have only left Africa as "the greatest development challenge facing the "[21]international community... If anything, these policies did not culminate in structural transformation of Africa's distorted economic and social structures, they failed to encourage sectoral linkages, strengthen the state and dominant classes, or improve local science and technology to promote productivity and encourage self-reliance.

As is by now quite obvious, the reform and developmental policies of the 1960s and 1970s merely consolidated the domination of African economies by foreign interests, their continuing concentration on cash crop production, and the reliance of the elites on the state for accumulation. The state, in the context of a weak and subservient dominant class emerged as the main employer, main contractor, main importer and source of seed capital for all types of businesses.
With a corrupt elite and an over expanded, inefficient state the rural areas

were neglected, agricultural output declined, the urban centers became overcrowded, the informal sector grew but was neglected, institutions deteriorated, the environment was abused and the economies were simply opened up for foreign manipulation and exploitation, in most instances through an unequal but lucrative alliance between local and foreign interests.

In addition to the responses above, African leaders saw regionalism as a major way out of their weaknesses and marginal location in the global system. If they pulled their economies and resources together they would be able to specialize and enjoy the benefits of economies of scale, regulate foreign investment, promote accumulation through the creation of a larger market, and recapture some of the lost cultural and social realities of African societies through the free flow of goods, services and persons across colonially drawn national boundaries. Unfortunately, once again, most of the regional integration schemes were of the hybrid and liberal constructs and were not structured to attack the structures of dependence, underdevelopment and foreign domination.

In addition to such serious structural deficiencies, the schemes were dominated by the elites and afflicted by inefficiency, petty jealousies, lack of resources, lack of the political will to implement policies, and conflicts between nationalistic economic programs and regionally-based agendas. As well, continuing dependence on tariff duties for revenues, inability to specialize and forge common approaches towards donors and foreign investors, failure to design specific policies to check domination by particular countries and to compensate weaker participants, ideological differences, and political instability and lack of regime and policy continuity in the majority of African states served to check possibilities for viable regional integration schemes.[22]

Hence regionalist schemes like the East African Community (EAC) , the West African Economic Community (CEAO) , Economic Community of West African States (ECOWAS) , and even the Southern African Development Coordinating Conference(SADCC) have disintegrated, become stagnant, or achieved very little. In spite of the declared hopes for establishing an African Common Market in AD2025 through the *Lagos Plan of Action* and *The Final Act of Lagos* and the 1991 adoption of an *African Economic Treaty* which is expected to convert Africa into a Common Market in AD2025, and lead to the establishment of a common monetary policy and the election of an African parliament, it is clear that like previous efforts, such grandiose and ambitious schemes will fail.[23] What with the deepening crisis of the region, declining foreign technical and financial support and the struggles by the state and its custodians to survive the constraints of domestic economic disaster and pressures in the evolving global order.

In the context of the failure of regional and national policies, African states had no options but to resort to the adoption of IMF and World Bank stabilization and adjustment policies in the 1980s. It is quite true that in practically every instance, African states approached the two organizations only when credit lines were closed, and suppliers and creditors insisted on a stabilization and adjustment package for further business. As well, donors and western governments began in the mid-1980s to demand not only economic restructuring but pluralist political engineering as pre-conditions for further foreign aid and other 15 technical support. The Fund and Bank practically took over the management of the financial and economic activities of the adjusting economies.

In spite of claims to the contrary by the World Bank, African countries, the OAU and ECA are agreed that structural adjustment programs, as conceived and implemented by the World Bank as a response to the region's crisis, have failed to stem the tide of deterioration. In the words of Richard Jolly, "it is clear that Africa's crisis continues. Africa's debt is still rising, average per capita incomes are still falling and the number in poverty... is still projected almost 50% by the end of the century."[24] Cuts in government expenditures have hardly affected the African elite and have had a devastating impact on efficiency, social services, and the relevance of the government.

Devaluation programs have made most currencies worthless, failed to attract foreign investors or improved trade in any significant way, and have ruined indigenous industries as spare parts, inputs and skilled labor became unaffordable. High and floating interest rates have simply eliminated or seriously weakened local business interests as they find it almost impossible to borrow or service their debts. It has increased speculation in money and increased the power of foreign capital which enjoys the backing of their corporate headquarters and access to foreign exchange. Privatization overlooks why the so-called government owned companies are not making profits nepotism, political interference, lack of accountability and so on and has tended to encourage the sale of public corporations to 16 foreign interests and/or their local representatives. Visible symbols and institutions of nationalism and self-reliance like airlines, communications facilities, banks and so on, have been sold to foreign interests in the name of privatization and the need to generate foreign exchange. Rapid privatization ignores the shortage of capital, technology, credible investors, and the need to be sensitive to the genuine needs of the people. Trade liberalization has removed all controls on imports and led to the flooding of African markets with cheap, poorly packaged, dangerous and outdated goods which in the context of devaluation, wage freeze and massive unemployment, are beyond the reach of the masses of the people.

Finally, the removal of subsidies from education, health and other social services has moved Africa back to the days of colonialism where only the expatriate community and a handful of African elites could afford the good schools, the best hospitals, and the very best amenities in the colony. As the OAU has noted:

> African economies were required to make ... adjustments and achieve economic growth in the face of severely compressed incomes and rising debt overhang. This is an impossible dilemma. Not surprisingly the results achieved have been mixed- while some countries have achieved significant results, many are still to reap the fruits of their effort in any meaningful way. The hardships caused by the decline in incomes were so severe that structural adjustment came to be associated with privation in several countries.[25]

Though in 1989, the World Bank moved in its report to acknowledge the political dimensions of the crisis and to prescribe decentralization, independence of the judiciary, political accountability, popular participation in decision-making, a check on waste and corruption, and the protection of vulnerable groups in the adjustment process, it was clear that the situation could no longer be contained through post-hoc, cosmetic and monetarist "shock treatments. " In a country like Zambia, copper prices continued to fall, foreign debts increased from 40 per cent of GDP in 1975 to 400 per cent of GDP in 1986 and annual scheduled debt service payment stood at $900 million or 95 per cent of all export earnings.

The implication was that if Zambia "paid its obligations, it would have no money at all for its vital imports, which are the basis of much of its economy, and which also include essentials like food, fertilizer, and medicines. So the government was in a position neither to adequately service its debt,, nor to provide the variety of essential services for health, education, agriculture, etc., at anywhere near the level the people required."[26] Finally in the Nigerian case, Sam Aluko, a prominent economist has argued that "Our economy is poorer today in production level than in 1986, even our agriculture. I have not seen anything gained from SAP. Our debt has become more difficult to pay. The rate of interest has risen so we cannot borrow money to do business ... SAP has destroyed the incentive to invest and produce. There are no new investment ....

Production has collapsed.".[27]

Beyond and/or complimenting these responses have been the United Nations Program of Action for African Economic Recovery and Development(UNPAAERRD) adopted in 1986 and abandoned in 1991; the African Priority Program for Economic Recovery 1986- 18 1990(APPER), which has since been overtaken by events; and the UN New Agenda for Development of Africa in the 1990s adopted in December 1991 which spells out a range of reforms required within Africa and the global economy to rescue the region from its present predicaments. These and other responses will make very minimal difference for Africa unless certain specific and broad changes occur at the levels of politics, power, production, and exchange relations.

Why African Economies Will Not Recover: The Way Out

What we have seen in Zaire, Somalia, the Sudan, Liberia, Togo, Mozambique, Angola and other parts of Africa show very clearly that further deterioration, even the disintegration of the state is possible any day. The events in Eastern Europe also show that ethnic conflicts are not peculiar to Africa and that the end of the cold war has unleashed new coalitions, contradictions and conflicts. As well, the redirection of interest, aid, and investment to Russia and parts of the Commonwealth of Independent States at the expense of Africa shows very vividly that Africa must seek an alternative route to growth and development; and that it would require serious restructurings at the level of politics and economy to take advantage of shrinking opportunities in the global system.

Edward Jaycox notes that "the 1990s will be a critical decade for Africa. The world is in the midst of fundamental change and the ideological blinkers which so greatly hampered economic development for so long have been taken off.[28] The Global 19 Coalition for Africa believes that "The danger now is that unless quick and forceful action is taken, the 1990s will not be a turning point in the region's history."[29] And the North South Roundtable has noted that "If Africa is unable to pull out of its crisis, the loss will be not only for another ten years, but of an entire generation, seriously retarding the continent's prospects for development well into the next century."[30] It becomes clear that there is global awareness of the tide of decay in Africa, especially sub-Saharan Africa.

Africa will NOT get out of its current crisis in so far as resource flows from the developed economies continues to decline; investors continue to divest and reinvest in Eastern Europe; commodity prices continue to slide; the UN remains under the tyranny of the Security Council and the General

Assembly grows increasingly powerless unable to sustain debates and put issues favorable to developing countries on the global agenda; and in so far as Africa remains unimportant in the global geo-strategic and economic calculations of the United States.[31]

This is important given the disintegration of the Soviet Union as a nation and super-power and the preoccupation of Russia with market reforms and political stability. In spite of frequent statements as to the importance of Africa to U.S. interests, the truth is that "American economic interests in Africa are marginal."[32] Most of U.S imports from Africa come from Nigeria, Angola, and South Africa, and consists mostly of oil particularly since the 1970s. Exports to Africa "have never accounted for a 20 substantial proportion of total U.S. exports ... U.S. economic interests there are concentrated in a few countries ... direct investment in Africa is also relatively unimportant.

No African nation ranks among the top twenty locations for U.S. investments. Total U.S. investments in Africa currently equals less than one-third of U.S. investment in Brazil alone.[33] If Africa is unimportant, and the cold war which determined and influenced U.S. interests in Africa is no more, it follows that Africans must map out an alternate agenda to survive in a global order dominated by the United States, with a United Nations which has limited   resources and so controlled by the hegemonic United States; and an international market with investors less interested in investing the region.

To be sure, low level infrastructural development, political instability, wars and violence, low purchasing power of the people, corruption, bureaucratic obstacles to doing business, low level returns on investment and the excessively high cost of business transactions, have all contributed to the region's poor place in global economic relations. Yet, in the majority of African states, there are only very unsteady and tentative moves away from these debilitating conditions.

In Togo, the state has been completely delegitimized and over 250,000 refugees have fled to neighboring states of Ghana and Benin. In Liberia, the war continues and the Nigeria-led West African Economic Community Monitoring Group (ECOMOG) has been unable to resolve the conflict which has claimed over 50,000 lives. In South Africa, massacres, violence, and tensions continue to obstruct negotiations for majority rule. In Mozambique, a 16-year civil war has made the country one of the least developed and backward states in the world, completely unattractive to any serious investor. In Angola, elections in September 1991 after a 17-year civil war did not satisfy the American and South African supported Jonas Savimbi who resorted to armed warfare after he lost the election.

Since then, thousands of Angolans have been killed in the renewed conflict. In the Sudan, the situation today, a precipitate of underdevelopment and conflict between the Christian South and Muslim North, is worse than the Somali situation. The drought of 1988-89 killed over 300,000 Sudanese.[34] In Rwanda, "civil war rages between the Tutsi, the former ruling class, and the Hutus, who overthrew them in 1973."[35] Uganda is ravaged by AIDS, and human rights abuses, especially in areas outside the control of National Resistance Army continues.

In Zaire, the corrupt and decadent Mobutu regime has refused to respect the decisions of the National Conference, and continues to hold on to power after bankrupting the economy. In countries like Nigeria, Senegal, Cameroon, and Kenya, in spite of some tentative steps towards political pluralism, the economies are in such a state, that it will take decades to get them back on track and to attract investors. To make matters worse, after relying heavily on repression and the suffocation of civil society to force monetarist IMF and World Bank prescriptions on their peoples, donors, creditors and Western powers have added "political conditionality" to the list of requirements for further aid to African states.[36]

African leaders are now caught in a very tight spot: can state structures used to exploit, repress, and intimidate the people in the process of implementing very difficult policies which impoverished and alienated the vast majority from the state, its agents and institutions, be used to mobilize them for democracy and empowerment?

The current response to the African crisis, along side economic restructuring, is political pluralism. This new prescription, largely of the western neo-liberal political models multi-parties, periodic election, separation of powers, the recognition and guarantee of basic freedoms and so on, has been endorsed by donors, creditors, the Western powers, the ECA, OAU and the World Bank. The ECA for instance has argued that recovery in Africa will be impossible without the popular support and full participation of the people, neither can the economic crisis be resolved and the "human and economic conditions improved without the full and effective contribution, creativity and popular enthusiasm of the vast majority of the people".[37] It also believes that "unless the structures, pattern and political context of the process of socioeconomic development are appropriately altered," Africa's economic and social deterioration will continue unabated.

To achieve this, the ECA proposed a more humane, people-centered, and democratic adjustment package and the "opening up of the political process to accommodate freedom of opinions, tolerate differences, accept consensus on issues as well as ensure the effective participation of the people and their organizations and 23 association."[38] Boutros-Ghali has also argued that "Unless democracy takes root, violence, coups d'etat, wars and general instability will recur, with an inevitable effect on socioeconomic development. This has been the case in many regions and countries of Africa ... Time and time again, all across Africa, hopeful steps towards development have stopped because of instability.

This cycle can be broken only through the growth of democratic practices.[39] As well, Edward Jaycox, summarizing the position of the World Bank which has called for popular participation, empowerment of the people, respect for human rights, decentralization of the government, independence of the judiciary, and the guarantees of constitutional rights for all citizens, added the need for accountability, transparency in procedures, predictability of actions and behavior, openness and reliable flow of information, and capacity building.[40]

At the 1991 review of UNPAAERD, donors and representatives of western governments were unanimous on the need for political pluralism as an important ingredient to the recovery process in Africa.   This was in line with the shift in the World Bank's policy in 1989, acknowledging the importance of political factors and contradictions in the region's deepening crisis. Scott Spangler, representing the United States argued that only few African governments "undertook serious and sustained economic reform." As a reward they "did receive special assistance and debt relief from many donors." He pointed out that "Africa needs to shift from a government-dominated approach to development to a private sector- 4 led approach .... Africa needs a basic restructuring and redirection of government. " To the United States, there was a direct relationship between "the strong movements in many African countries toward democratization, which we believe will lead to better governance and fiscal accountability."[41] Robert Van Shaik, representing the European Community was clear on the fact that "Good governance and democracy form two essential preconditions for sustainable development."[42] The Japanese Ambassador to the UN, Yoshio Hatano called on African governments and leaders to strive to "achieve the widest possible participation of their people in the development process," as this would "encourage them to continue to promote democratization, respect for human rights, and the principles of good governance and accountability."[43]

It is obvious therefore, that the issue of democracy has become a fundamental aspect of prescriptions for Africa's recovery. Yet, democracy is seen primarily in terms of the ability to replicate western models in the context of market reforms. It has been quite easy for African leaders, under pressure from the West, lenders, and donors, to meet with the basic requirements and demands of pluralism by allowing the formation of political parties, open elections, and the operation of parliaments. But as we have seen in Kenya and Ghana, such moves have changed nothing. The incumbents have been returned to office with little dif faculty. They have manipulated the electoral processes, exploited the power of incumbency, and capitalized on the factionalization, fractionalization, opportunism and weaknesses of the opposition.

One can reach the safe conclusion that in so far as there is crass personalization of the struggle for democracy, and in so far as the opposition remains divided and weak, the political landscape in Africa will experience some superficial changes but no revolution. Yet, a serious and far-reaching political revolution in the content and context of politics is what is urgently required to create the necessary political terrain for economic and social reforms to succeed:

> ... given the socioeconomic conditions of Africa and the fact that up to 80 per cent of Africa's working people are peasants, multipartyism is more likely than not, in the first instance, to lead to conservative victories, and a multi-coloured cloak of legitimacy. Thus the multi-party state is unlikely to be any more responsive to either the needs or expressed wishes of the majority of Africa's population than the one party or military states have been .... To date multi-party elections in Africa have produced no fundamental change in Senegal, Gabon or Cote d'Ivoire. "[44]

It is to the need for "fundamental change" in the content and direction of politics in Africa that the *African Charter for Popular Participation* is directed. Adopted in Arusha, Tanzania in 1990, it has since been endorsed by the OAU and the UN as a basis for reorganizing the political terrain in Africa, empowering the people, their communities and organizations, guaranteeing basic freedoms and rights, and determining the responsibilities of popular organization, governments, and the international community in the democratization process.

Rather than focus on the mere indicators of *democracy*, the Charter directs attention at the salience of *democratization* by emphasizing human and people-centered development, mass mobilization, respect for human rights, accountability of the leadership, the democratization of public institutions, the involvement of the people in decision making, the provision of basic human needs, and the transformation of existing social, political and economic relations in a more pro-people direction.

As one of the most important documents to have come out of Africa in recent times (amongst the plethora of declarations, Charters and so on), it is amazing that African leaders have referred to it only glibly or completely ignored it though at the levels of the OAU and UN they have endorsed the Charter.

This is the more amazing given the very open pressures from the World Bank, donors and western governments on the need for political pluralism, human rights, accountability, and popular participation. African leaders have been told in very clear terms that if they "cannot demonstrate good governance, and a measure of development progress, the window of external support for Africa will close, donors will shift their assistance to more promising regions- and Africa will be further marginalized in the world."[45]

It is of course possible to argue that a drastic cut in foreign aid and some marginalization will be very good for Africa. After all, decades of dependence on foreign aid had very limited positive effect on the quality of life of the vast majority of Africans. The billions of dollars received in foreign aid went to subsidize military purchases, elite tastes, and provided resources for corrupt and irresponsible leaders to become arrogant, suffocate civil society, refuse to reach some accommodation with other constituencies, and to lubricate the harsh edges of mismanagement and deepening class contradictions. marginalization of course will enable African leaders to see the hand writing on the world, expose them to the realities of the emerging global order, reduce their power vis-a-vis the masses and their organizations, and force on the leaders and the people an urgent need to reconceptualize their methods of politics, models of development, appreciate the specificities of their respective social formations, look inwards for perspectives and prescriptions for authentic endogenous development. It is only in the context of declining foreign aid, reduced military intervention and manipulation with the end of the cold war, and declining investment that African leaders, left high and dry on the shores of the evolving international division of labor will realize that if "Africa does not begin to grow quickly now, it faces the prospect of never being able to catch up with the dynamic economies of the West and increasing parts of the Third World. In addition, if Africa continues to stagnate, there is probably no chance for political reform, environmental improvement, decreased poverty, and all of the other goals that everyone hopes for Africa."[46]

The African Charter has outlined the required reforms needed to put Africa on an alternative path to growth, development and democracy. In its prescriptions at the level of the people, it calls for the establishment of "independent people's organizations at various levels that are genuinely grass-root, voluntary, democratically administered and self-reliant and that are rooted in the tradition and culture of the society so as to ensure community empowerment and self -development."[47] African leaders have been able to appropriate the institutions, powers and resources of the state for decades because civil society was weak, fragmented, and dominated by the world-views of the elites.

The only way to break the cycle of corruption, repression, intimidation, mismanagement, the tenacity to office and the reproduction of undemocratic attitudes and actions is through the creation and empowerment of people's organizations and their direct involvement in politics. The document insists that African governments must "yield space to the people, without which popular participation will be difficult to achieve. Too often, the social base of power and decision-making are too narrow. Hence the urgent need to broaden these; to galvanize and tap the people's energy and commitment; and to promote political accountability by the state to the people."[48]

A new partnership between the state and the people is required to improve the conditions of women, rural people, check armed conflicts, protect the people's basic human rights, and promote popular participation and development. Without doubt, this is the only way to stop the brain drain, create an environment to attract investors and donors, encourage creativity, understanding and tolerance amongst the people, encourage the hundreds of thousands of Africans abroad to return home, and put the state in a position to regulate or control foreign investors and whip some discipline into the ranks of the elites.

The international community is enjoined to support "indigenous efforts which promote the emergence of a democratic environment and facilitate participation and empowerment;" while the UN system is called upon to "promote the application of justice in international economic relations, the defense of human rights, the maintenance of peace...." To be sure, international responses will be dependent on the extent of visible commitment to genuine democratization, economic reforms, and empowerment of the people and their communities. To keep complaining about the evils of the global capitalist system will be nothing new.

The truth is that the international system is structured to serve the interests of the more integrated, productive, stable, and powerful nations. No serious investor will divert resources to countries like Togo, Malawi, Sudan, Somalia, Angola or Mozambique when from all indicators the state and dominant elites are hardly in a position to guarantee the safety and security of investments and investors, and the courts can hardly enforce or protect contracts. The Charter also includes specific prescriptions for

NGOs and VDOS, the media and communication, women's organizations, organized labor, and youths, students and their organizations. At all levels the emphasis in on accountability, transparency, mobilization, participation, empowerment, and democracy and democratization.

Perhaps, the most significant contribution of The Charter, which puts it ahead of other responses is that it outlines specific ways in which popular participation in Africa can be monitored. These include the literacy rate, freedom of association, representation of the people and their organizations in national bodies, the rule of law and social and economic justice, environmental policies, freedom of the press and media, "number and scope of grassroots organizations with effective participation in development activities," the empowerment of women through the implementation of the 1989 Abuja Declaration on Women, political accountability of leadership at all levels, and decentralization of decision-making processes and institutions.[49]

The document ends by suggesting that the implementation of its recommendations be monitored at the national level by a machinery composed of representatives of the government, trade unions, women's organizations, NGOS, grass-roots and youth and student organizations. At the regional level, the Charter recommends a joint OAU/ECA Regional Monitoring Machinery with representatives from a network of popular groups. To be sure, there are glaring loopholes in the Charter. It is weak on economic prescriptions; it assumes that all so-called grassroot organizations are necessarily progressive and democratic; it assumes that the very same leaders who have spent decades looting their respective treasuries and asphyxiating civil society will suddenly make concessions to popular groups; it does not spell out sanctions to be imposed on nations which endorse but refuse to implement its prescriptions; it fails to define the status and autonomy of the monitoring agencies; and it does not place before the African people a credible agenda for political reconstruction, especially in the context of recalcitrant leadership as is the case in Zaire and Malawi.

Yet, it is a starting point for recognizing what is actually required for Africa's economic recovery: the creation of an "enabling environment" for investment, creativity, unity, efficient management of resources, accountability, sacrifice, and political tolerance. As Adebayo Adedeji noted in his closing statement at the 1990 International Conference on Popular Participation in the Recovery and Development Process in Africa where the Charter was adopted:

Africa needs fundamental change and transformation, not just adjustment.

The change and transformation required are not just narrow, economistic and mechanical ones. They are broader and fundamental changes that will bring about, over time, the new Africa of our vision where there is development and economic justice, not just growth; where there is democracy and accountability not despotism, authoritarianism and kleptocracy; and where the governed and their governments are moving hand-in-hand in the promotion of the common good, and where it is the will of the people rather than the wishes of one person or a group of 50 persons, however powerful, that prevails.[50]

It is interesting to note that new initiatives, debates, alignment and realignment of political forces are taking place all over Africa. In spite of the current fluid state of affairs at the economic and political fronts, the truth is that it will be impossible to stop the tide of change. The end of the cold war has reduced the strategic value of many African states and thus eliminated the need to provide political, financial, and military support to repressive leaders. Increasing economic crisis in the western economies in influencing an inward looking brand of politics and a selective allocation of foreign aid to developing formations. There is also a new interest in Eastern Europe partly to completely eliminate the vestiges of communism, but also to exploit the new markets of that region. All these will create more political and ideological spaces in Africa which popular forces can exploit to influence and determine the direction of politics.

There is no doubt that the lack of a powerful constituency for Africa in Europe and North America, the loss of the UN as a fora to push pro-African programs in the context of unquestionable domination of global strategic and political relations by the United States, and the emergence of trade blocs in the Pacific Rim, Europe, and North America, will reduce Africa's room for manoeuver in the global system. These inhibitions will only weaken Africa's leaders and strengthen advocates of self-reliance, regional autonomy, and popular control of the content and context of politics.

If African states are serious about recovery in the 1990s, it would be evidenced in the way and manner they go about political and economic restructuring in order to unleash new and, powerful forces of production in a context of a strengthened civil society and popular participation in the political process. Anything short of this agenda will culminate in the reproduction of the present crisis and the peripheralization of the region in the international division of labor.

84   *Contemporary African Politics:*

Notes

1. The Global Coalition for Africa, *African Social and Economic Trends-1992 Annual Report* (Washington, DC: The Global Coalition for Africa, November 1992), p.3 and p. 4.
2 General Ibrahim Babangida, Address at the 46th Session of the United Nations General Assembly in his capacity as Chairman, The organization of African Unity, New York, October 4, 1991.
3. Boutros-Ghali, "Overcoming the Crisis in Development Cooperation," Address to the Conference on Global Development Cooperation, The Carter Center, Atlanta, Georgia, 4 December 1992.
4. Africa's marginalization has been acknowledged by the UN, ECA and OAU.   See for instance, "Conference to Counter Africals marginalization," *Africa Recovery* Vol. 6 (2) (August 1992).
5. There is new direction of scholarship which acknowledges external dimensions of the African crisis but sees the solutions as arising first, from radical internal restructuring.   See Salim Lone, "Africa Focuses on Internal Weaknesses," *Africa Recovery* Vol. 6 (4) (December 1992-February 1993), and Ernest Harsch, "African Reforms Under the Spotlight," *Africa Recovery* Vol 6 (2) (August 1993).
6. See the very useful works of Issa Shivji, Dan Nabudere, Claude Ake, Bade Onimode, Walter Rodney, Segun Osoba, Samir Amin, Ade Ajayi, obaro Ikime, Julius Nyerere, Kwame Nkrumah and a host of others who have written on Africa's historical experience and the implication for contemporary social, political, and economic relations.
7. See Economic commission for Africa, *Economic Report on Africa 1990* (Addis Ababa: ECA Secretariat, 1990).
8 See World Bank, *Sub-Saharan Africa: From Crisis to Sustainable Growth- A Long-Term Perspective Study* (Washington, DC: World Bank, 1989).
9. See Organization of African Unity, *Lagos Plan of Action for the Economic Development of Africa 1980-2000* (Geneva: International Institute for Labour Studies, 1981). In the words of the OAU, "Africa is unable to point to any significant growth rate, or satisfactory index of general well-being, in the past 20 years." (P.').
10. Edward P. Jaycox, *The Challenges of African Development* (Washington, DC: The World Bank, 1992), p. p.15.
11. Boubakar Diaby-Ouattara, "Overview" in The Global Coalition for Africa, *African Social and Economic Trends ...* op. cit., p.2.
12. Ibid, p. 6.
13. ibid, pp. 6-7.

14.Michael Chege, "Remembering Africa," *Foreign Affairs* Vol. 71 (1)(1991-92), p.157.

15.Economic Commission for Africa, *African Charter for Popular Participation in Development and Transformation* (Addis Ababa: ECA, 1990), p. 17.

16.See John Ravenhill (ed.), *Africa in Economic Crisis* (London: Macmillan, 1986); Bonnie Campbell and John Loxley (eds.), *Structural Adiustment in Africa* (London: Macmillan) ; and Timothy M. Shaw, "Africa's Conjuncture: From Structural Adjustment to Self-Reliance," *Dalhousie Review* Vol. 68 (1-2) (Spring-Summer 1988).

17.See Carol Lancaster, "Economic Restructuring in Africa," *Current History* Vol. 88 (538) (May 1989) ; Adebayo Adedeji, "The African Challenges in the 1990s: New Perspectives for Development," *Indian Journal of Social Science* (3) (1990) ; and Robert Browne, "The Continuing Debate on African Development," *TransAfrica Forum* Vol. 7 (2) (Summer 1990).

18.Economic Commission for Africa, *African Charter* op. cit., p. 19.

19. "UMPAAERD Speeches Debate Issues of Debt, Governance, and Aid Flows," *Africa Recovery* Vol. 5 (4) (December 1991), p.24.

20.Layashi Yaker, Keynote Address at the Conference on "Africa in Transition: Challenges and Opportunities," Thunderbird, AGSIM, Glendale, Arizona, 18-20 February, 1993.

21.Edward Jaycox, *The Challenges of African Development* op. cit., p.14.

22. See Julius 0. Ihonvbere, "Towards A Re-Conceptualization of Integration Theory in Peripheral Regions- The Case of ECOWAS" *ODU; A Journal of West African Studies* (24) (July 1983) ; Timothy M. Shaw, "Africa's Crisis: Debate and Dialectics Over Alternative Development Strategies for the Continent," *Alternatives* Vol. 9 (1) (June 1988) ; and Ralph I. Onwuka and Amadu Sesay (eds.), *The Future of Regionalism in Africa* (London: Macmillan, 1985).

23. See Julius 0. Ihonvbere, "Towards an African Common Market in AD 2025?: The African Crisis, Regionalism and Prospects for Recovery." Paper presented at the International conference on Africa and Eastern Europe: Lessons and Parallels, Queen's University, Kingston, Ontario, Canada., April 12-13, 1992.

24. Ibid

25. See OAU, Lagos Plan of Action for Economic Development of Africa 1980-2000 *opcit.*

26. ECA African Charter *opcit*

27. Ibid

28. Edward Jaycox *opcit* p.18
29. The Global Coalition for Africa *opcit*
30. Julius Ihonvbere (1983) *opcit*
31. Boutros Ghali (1992)
32. ibid.
33. ECA Report, 1990.
34. Julius Ihonvbere (1992)opcit.
35. ibid.
36. See World Bank Study.(1989)*opcit*.
37. ECA Report (1990) *opci*t.
38. Ibid
39. Ibid
40. Edward Jaycox (1992)*opcit*
41. Robert Brown (1990)
42. Ibid
43. Julius Ihonvbere (1992)*opcit*
44. ECA (1990)*opcit*.
45. World Bank Study(1989)*opci*t
46. Ibid
47. See OAU Lagos Plan of Action.*opcit*.
48. Ibid
49. Ibid.
50. ECA(1990) *opcit*.

PART II : Political Transition In Comparative Perspective.

Democratization in Africa continue to face a daunting array of obstacles but in some cases efforts are being made to build necessary political institutions capable of sustaining this process. While efforts in some countries have failed, some countries have become the icon of what democracy could bring . In some , political stability has provided people some degree of hope, while the process in others has failed to stem violence. The failure in many continue to trouble students of African politics, especially in Nigeria where recently the military is facing the greatest challenge to its hold on political power brought about by the sudden death of the autocrat General Sanni Abacha and the imprisoned winner of the Nigerian 1993 Presidential election, Chief Moshood Abiola (June 8 and July 7, 1998 respectively) .

In Part two ,four case study will be presented in an attempt to identify the problems and prospects of democratization in Africa. The Ugandan model and the Namibian democratic transition to nationhood presents a positive prospect while the South African example remain largely a symbolic inspiration for democratic governance but bedevil with uncertainties and violence. The Nigerian example is a chronic case of all that is wrong with democratic transition in Africa- an over-politicized military institution, a multi-ethnic society and a corrupt and kleptomania leadership.

Chapter 5

Democratic Representation: A Ugandan Model

Thomas O'hara

Within the last generation, the world's political landscape has undergone dramatic changes. Much political analysis has been directed to the end of the cold war, the breakup of communism, and the attempts of Eastern European societies to develop into democratic states. The road to democracy has been perilous indeed. However, to the South of Europe, in Africa, for decades societies have been trying to break away not from the shackles of communism, but colonialism. There too the road to democracy has been tricky. History seems to demonstrate that moving away from colonial domination has been no easier than moving away from Communist domination.

This chapter represents a case presentation of one of those countries struggling to define democracy for itself - Uganda. In order to examine the model of democracy being implemented in Uganda today, it is very important to understand the context for Ugandan political development. Thus, a quick section on political history is followed by a section describing the unique role of religion in Ugandan politics. It can be fairly argued that religious sectarianism gave birth to the formation of political parties in Uganda. Yet, the present model of democracy in Uganda puts an end to a multiparty approach to democracy and that new model is discussed in the sections that highlight the political philosophy of the present President Yoweri Museveni, the making of the constitution, and the response of the international community (especially the United States). Museveni's model presents a new challenge to the Western style multi party democratic framework.

Political History

Late in the 19th century Uganda, like much of East Africa, was artificially created without respect to tribal boundaries. Over forty tribes were arbitrarily pulled together in the same political unit. Uganda was under British control and the British were eager to stamp as much of their social -political culture as they could on the Ugandan territory. Within the territory of Uganda they found one tribe - the Buganda- that possessed a highly developed monarchical system. Such a monarchical system, easily understood by the British, was ready made for implementation of British rule. Such a centralized monarchy facilitated the British objective of control over this part of Africa. So the Buganda became the favored tribe and for years to come the Buganda had the most economic and political clout in Uganda. In 1962 the London Conference was called for the purposes of laying groundwork for an independent Ugandan State.

The political power was transferred to the Kabaka (King) of the Buganda and his allies in a political party called the UPC. The leader of that party, Milton Obote, was named Prime Minister of this new country. Though Buganda was only part of the larger Uganda, it was allowed to keep its monarchical system and the new nation's capital, Kampala, was situated in the Bugandan kingdom. However from the time of 1962 to 1986, Ugandan political history consisted mostly of political instability and internal war. The transition of power from colonial to independent rule was not easy. The government inherited an extensive bureaucracy created by the British but had a great deal of difficulty managing it effectively. The economy suffered through skyrocketing inflation.

Corruption in government and the private sector threatened to overwhelm the economy. As a result, internal dissension and resistance to the government increased and political instability was becoming most obvious. Obote tried to maintain power by becoming increasingly autocratic. The strategy only alienated him more and in 1966 as political struggles mounted for Obote, the alliance between the monarchy and his UPC party fell apart. Obote abrogated the 1962 constitution that recognized the monarchy and forced the Kabaka into exile in London. Under increasing pressure and with the economy sliding, Obote increased yet again his strongman tactics to maintain power.

Finally his actions led to a coup in 1971 by his chief Military Commander Idi Amin, successfully overthrowing the Obote government. Yet Amin faced the same instability and simply followed the strategy of Obote. In fact, he exacerbated the problem as he conducted his reign of terror killing hundreds of thousands of Ugandans. He also effectively destroyed the economy by expelling the Asian business community. As Amin followed more and more dictatorial policies his downfall became inevitable when he decided to invade a foreign country. He committed a tactical blunder by invading Tanzania. Julius Nyerere, then President of Tanzania, was a stanch opponent of Amin and he was only too happy to oblige in war. The Tanzanian army invaded Uganda, defeating Amin's Army. Amin was forced into exile and for the time being Tanzania supervised a transition government.

After the downfall of Amin and a temporary care taker government, there was a national election for a new government in 1980. To this point the only political party that governed was the UPC. However, an opposition party, the Democratic Party, DP, seemed to be gaining momentum. In fact in 1980 the DP was confident of electoral victory. It's candidate, Paul Ssemogerere, was a very popular figure throughout Uganda. It appeared they would indeed win, but after several days and presumed rigging of the vote, Milton Obote and the UPC were returned to power for a second time. This apparent stealing of the elections only infuriated and divided the country once again and under Obote II political tension and hostility within the country increased.

In the early 1980's the present President, Yoweri Museveni and his army, the National Resistance Army, NRA, began a rebel movement against the Obote government and a long and costly Civil War ensued. In a bitter five year struggle more than a half million Ugandans were killed and that many fled the country. Chaos reigned throughout this brutal period of oppression. Finally, in 1986, Museveni's National Resistance Army, NRA, overcame government forces and swept into Kampala taking control of the government. Uganda had suffered greatly; in these brutal regimes of Obote and Amin nearly a million Ugandans were killed. Though seizing government by force, Museveni promised to restore order and democracy to Ugandans; however, Amin and Obote had made similar promises. Museveni promised to be different; Ugandans once again held their breath.

Religion As A Party Building Factor In Ugandan Politics

One cannot understand Ugandan politics without first examining the crucial link between religion and the political structure of Uganda. From colonial days the country was fiercely divided on tribal and religious grounds. In fact, it is rather clear that at the time of independence these sectarian divisions laid the basis for competing political parties, the

Democratic Party (DP) and the Ugandan People's Congress, (UPC). The parties, organized on tribal and religious differences, gave formal political recognition to and in fact intensified the divisions within Ugandan society. One of the leading scholars on the question of religion and politics in Uganda was Dan Mudoola, a prominent political scientist who studied interest group influence on the formation of political parties in Uganda.(1) According to Mudoola religious groups were most critical to the formation of political parties. Shortly after Mudoola published his monumental study in the early 1990's, he was assassinated by unknown assailants. But before his death he made a most significant contribution to the literature on party formation by documenting that from colonial days the impact of the churches on politics was most significant. In some way, missionaries were part were of the colonization process, bringing Western religion to complement Western cultural and political values. Of course the state religion of England was the Church of England; so before long the King of Buganda, the Kabaka, and his court became members of the newly established Church of Uganda. As the King became Protestant, so did the vast majority of chiefs in the Buganda Kingdom. Even though Catholic missionaries were also very active, converting many of the general populace to the Catholic faith, the political leadership was solidly Protestant.

In the mid twentieth century, Catholics began to approach the numerical majority even though they did not hold the political power. Mudoola makes the argument that this sense of political marginalization led Catholics to organize socially and politically. In the social arena, Catholics developed their own extensive school system providing them with a formal institution to propagate its religious- cultural message. On the political front, a new political party was born, the Democratic Party or the DP, which championed the political and social grievances of the Catholic community. In Mudoola's terms, " the DP became the political-cultural base for the Catholic Church in Uganda." The Protestant political elite also coalesced around the other main political party, the Ugandan Peoples Congress, the UPC. In Mudoola's analysis, the UPC became the Protestant attempt to contain the DP and the Catholics. When Amin, a Muslim, became president, Muslims throughout the country celebrated. Mudoola reports that at the central mosque in Kampala a colorful ceremony attended by thousands of Moslems urged all in attendance to "rally behind our Savior Major General Idi Amin." Amin attempted to play his religious card as had been the history of other political leaders in Ugandan politics. In his tenure Amin attempted to develop closer ties with Islamic countries and massive amounts of foreign aid from Islamic countries came to Uganda in support of the new Muslim leader. He attempted to replace the Christian notion of Sunday as the national free day for religious worship to Friday so that Muslims would be free from work and commercial engagements. In the end, both days were declared national holidays.

He was even able to capitalize on a simmering political split within the Muslim community. When Obote ruled there were many Muslims, mostly younger and more doctrinaire, who wanted to follow a pattern similar to that of the Catholics, that is, keeping distance from the government. On the other hand, more established and older Muslims saw the practicality of working with Obote. They formed an organization, the National Association for the Advancement of Muslims, NAAM, for the purpose of " cooperating with the government and promoting unity among Moslems." With the establishment of this group, the younger and more militant Moslems were politically alienated. It is this group of more radical Muslims that Amin turned to for help and who served as principal support to him. However, despite this religious support, Amin's reign of terror led to his inevitable downfall and after the Tanzanians overcame him, he was sent off to exile.

In the election for a new government in 1980 the DP was now in a position to come to power. The DP candidate, Paul Ssemogerere, a Catholic, seemed to be the one to lead Uganda away from it's past and into a new future. However, after the rigging of the election and the return of Obote and the UPC to power, the Catholics were more furious than ever and in Mudoola's term were once again "marginalized." In 1986 when Museveni and his rebel army were successful in overthrowing the Obote and UPC government, many Catholics were once again happy to see the downfall of Obote. It is clear that once the NRM came to power, they were anxious to see an end to the sectarian struggles that had simmered and festered for the previous two decades.

Clearly they saw religion at the base of such divisions. The Minister of State for Education stated, " We appeal to all Ugandans to desist from mixing religion with politics. We urge all religious leaders to refrain from preaching a religion of hatred and division within society. This division was first brought about by colonial rulers who preached division in the churches and unfortunately our political parties were based on religion in that Protestants were UPC and Catholics were DP." (2) Museveni himself sounded a similar theme when he stated, " In our multi religious countries we cannot afford to allow religion a role in politics because if we do there will be increasing conflict and confrontation as all religious groups vie for power. As I speak a bitter civil war is going on in one of our neighboring countries because religion was brought into politics, one religious group trying to impose its doctrine on others, bringing death and misery to millions of people." (3)   Museveni's attempt to downplay the role of religion in politics is but a part of his overall political philosophy.

The Political Philosophy Of President Museveni.

While Museveni was in the bush fighting government troops for control of the country, he was developing his political philosophy which was the philosophy of his National Resistance Movement. The document outlining his philosophy became known as the NRM Ten Point Programme and it served as the framework for his government. The document promised a restoration of democracy and security, consolidation of national unity and elimination of sectarianism, restoration of the economy and infrastructure, and assistance to Ugandans displaced by the long years of war.

In his swearing in address on January 29, 1986, he elaborated on some of these points. When he spoke of democracy, he announced an elaborate nation wide system of Resistance Committees in each village. These committees represented a new model of grass roots type of government at the local level. As he stated, " These committees will have a lot of power. You cannot join the army or the police without being cleared by the village committee. You must get a recommendation from the people in your village saying you are not a rogue." (4) He also made it very clear that he was out to minimize the tribal and religious divisions that often led to so much previous instability and violence.

In that same inaugural address he stated, " Past regimes have used sectarianism to divide people along religious and tribal lines. But why should religion be considered a political matter? Religious matters are between you and your God. Thus the Movement does not tolerate religious and tribal divisions, or divisions along party lines such as UPC and DP (the two main political parties)." (5) A few days later, meeting elders of a village he stated, "You need to establish a Resistance Committee here. The NRM is not a party like the DP or UPC. Every Ugandan should join the National Resistance Movement to restore the country to normalcy. This is the aim and the purpose of the NRM: to unite everybody in order to solve this national crisis which is before us.

Once we have solved our national crisis, if you want to go back to your politics of dividing the country, you can do so after the interim period. We shall hand it over to you. If you want to tear it up again, it is up to you. In the meantime, however, it is our view that we must suspend the politics of the DP and UPC and practice the politics of unity for the first time in the history of our country." (6)

Thus it was clear from the outset that Museveni was going to attempt democracy in a different way than though the classical multi party democracy of the West. His idea of democracy centered on mass participation at the local level and representative committees at village and district levels and finally a national parliament; however all run within the context of The National Resistance Movement, devoid of organized parties. On the ninth anniversary of his government Museveni reflected back on the beginnings, " Those of you who are old enough know the tensions created in the villages by the unprincipled divisions of the 1960's, 70's and early 80's. The hemorrhage of life that engulfed Uganda between 1966 and 1986 had its genesis in sectarianism. We endeavored to show the confluence of interests among our people irrespective of party, tribe or religion."(7)

Museveni wanted such broad based support because he had ambitious plans. Foremost among those plans was to rebuild the country economically. Thus, point number 4 of his 10 Point Programme was to " Build an Independent, Integrated and Self Sustaining National Economy." He called for diversification of crops in the agriculture sector, production of import substitutes especially for basic consumer goods, processing of export raw materials so as to raise the value, and the building of basic industries. He began a program to invite back the Asians that Amin had expelled, returning their property to them in hopes they would bring new life into the devastated economy. At the same time he became a vigorous supporter of foreign investment in a new Uganda and met with a fair amount of success. His stated aim was to rebuild a middle class.

Ever aware of ways to break up the sectarianism in Uganda he stated, " If there is a middle class, it will cut across ethnic lines."(8) Obviously his deep belief was that economic progress would also help meet a political goal of national unity that would overcome sectarian, tribal and religious divisions. He drastically curtailed the civil service and thus attempted to deal with government corruption that was often paralyzing the economy. Similarly, he began the process of downsizing the army and its enormous budget. He granted political amnesty to those in exile who were willing to come back and rebuild Uganda, even encouraging rebels who fought against his army. He increased freedom of the press and established a Human Rights Commission to attempt to deal with the atrocities created in the previous 15 years. But it was clear that he was not interested in having protracted investigations and trials. He stated, " We thought trying to punish everybody would be an endless process." (9) His overwhelming desire was to unify and move forward economically.

In fact, he made enormous economic progress. Asians began returning, foreign investment increased, international governments and the IMF began assistance and long term loan programs. Industries sprouted up, even tourism began. By the mid 1990's Uganda became the fastest growing economy in East Africa and one of the fastest growing on the continent. From May 1987, the economy has been growing at an average of 6.5% per annum and inflation has been reduced from 250% in 1987 to 6.0% currently. Industrial production has been increasing at about 20% a year. The number of vehicles in the country increased from 26, 00 in 1987 to 74, 000 in 1994. Export revenues have tripled from 1986 to 96. Real GDP growth has tripled in these years, from 1.5% to 4.5%. (10) Clearly, Museveni saw economic progress as a way to political stability.

In fact even though his first point of the Ten point programme calls for " Restoration of Democracy", it is quickly asserted within that goal, "Although the National Resistance Movement believes in free and fair elections held at regular intervals, it asserts that democracy cannot be meaningful without a reasonable standard of living for all people." (11)

The Making Of The Constitution

Having established his government through force, Museveni and the NRM needed to legitimize their power. It was clear from the outset that his form of democracy would be somewhat unique. The first task was for the country to draw up a new constitution. He did not move into this process immediately. Three years after taking power, in February of 1989, he established a 21 member Constitutional Commission for the purpose of drafting a proposed national constitution that would be debated by a larger elected body, the Constituent Assembly. The Constitutional Commission was broadly representative of the Ugandan political landscape. It contained members of the NRM, the military, the clergy, and both major political parties, the DP and the UPC.

From all accounts this commission took its task quite seriously. Said one member of the commission, " It took a while for the individual commissioners to learn that it couldn't be a vehicle for party interests. But once that was learned, they sought the common view." Said a military member of the commission, "The old constitutions were controversial and could not be the basis for peace. We wanted to rethink the constitutional order, which has been in crisis since 1962. We believed that if we created a constitution based on national consensus, it would be a stronger foundation for stability."(12)

The commission was most deliberate in its work. Over a four year period, the commission visited every district and all 800 counties of Uganda to solicit popular opinion on a new constitution. In addition to oral testimony it received 16, 500 written memoranda from civic groups, churches, local governments, and NGO's. This wide consultation process drew favorable international reaction. Anthony Reagan, an Australian Constitutional lawyer attached to the commission stated, "This draft constitution has been written after an astounding and unparalleled rate of popular participation." (13)

In March of 1994 elections were held for the Constituent Assembly that was to debate and ultimately ratify the draft constitution. The constituent assembly consisted of 288 members, 214 elected directly at the local levels. Fifty six were elected or appointed by special interest groups, trade unions, the army, youth, women, and the disabled. Ten were appointed directly by President Museveni, and each party which contested the last nationwide election was allotted two additional delegates. Although the election law for the Constituent Assembly stated that elections were to be held without reference to political parties, tribe, or religion, it was rather clear who was running to support and ratify the new constitution and who was running to oppose it.

The most crucial aspect of the constitution was the provision that extended the life of the NRM government for five more years, in effect barring parties from contesting a national election for Parliament or President. Threfore the election to this ratifying constitution was seen as a referendum on the NRM and Museveni's no party approach to government. There was a uniform campaigning process; candidates met the electorate together in village forums to make their presentations and to field questions. Once again the mass participation was impressive; 87% of all registered voters voted. There were 200 international observers and over 10,000 local monitors. The result was a clear victory for Museveni and the NRM. Over 2/3 of the delegates elected were pledged to support the new constitution which extended the life of the NRM for five more years.

When the Constituent Assembly began its work, the battle lines were clearly drawn. Movement delegates wanted to ensure that the movement was given a chance to operate the government, free of interference from the parties. It was clearly felt that the parties would once again capitalize on tribal and religious cleavages and destroy the unity that movementists felt they were creating within the country. Therefore controversial provisions of the draft constitution were meant to entrench the movement and drastically limit the effectiveness of political parties.   Article 94 of the Constitution provided that the Movement, open to all Ugandan citizens, would constitute the political organization of the government. Articles 96 and 97 allowed for the existence of political parties but without the ability to "endorse, sponsor, offer a platform to, or in any way campaign for or against a candidate for any public election while the movement is in existence." The parties also had to have a "national character, and membership shall not be based on ethnic, religious, district, or other sectional basis." A further provision stated that "the parties's emblem, color, motto or any other symbol has no ethnic, religious, or other sectional connotation." The life of the movement was to be guaranteed for at least five years after the election of the President under the Constitution. In the fifth year of the President's term a national referendum would be held " to determine whether or not the movement should continue in existence or whether the system of representation through political parties should be adopted in place of the movement."(Article 98 of Draft Constitution.)

The multipartyists, both DP and UPC followers, countered that in the first five years there should be a coalition government of both movement and multipartyists. They rejected the marginalization of parties claiming, " political parties are a birth right that should not be negotiated" (14) The movementists did not budge, contending that after 5 years of the movement the people could decide if they wanted to return to multi parties. Said one movement delegate, " We have been directly elected to this assembly and we were under instructions from our constituents to advocate for the continuation of the movement system. There is no way we could go back and tell the people we have brought back parties without consulting them." (15) For the multiparty supporters, every attempt to defeat the controversial articles failed. Finally in utter futility , 64 multiparty delegates walked out of the Assembly stating that the constitution " extends a monolithic system and stifles a matter of fundamental principle." (16)

Reaction to the walkout was swift. An editorial in the National newspaper *The New Vision*, stated, " The rulership of parties in Uganda is tainted with gross abuse of human rights, political intolerance and unequaled mismanagement of the country. The murderers of yesterday seemed to be telling the Assembly of the sanctity of human rights." (17) Another editorial questioned, " Is the politics of hatred and anger a permanent feature of our statehood? It is incredible that despite all the humiliation and tyranny the people of Uganda have gone through, the time of Obote and Amin that wrecked this country, attempts by the movement to reassemble the population from the tyranny of the past have been poisoned by the UPC supporters in the Assembly. " (18)

It is with this background that the constitution was finally ratified by the Constituent Assembly. In order to prevent the type of sectarian politics that led to chaos, the delegates insisted on the controversial provisions. The role of political parties would be minimalized in the new government and their political power greatly reduced. They extended the life of the movement for five years though they allowed for an opening of the process in the latter stages. The final document states that two years before the end of the term, campaigning could begin for support of one of three options for the next government (1) The movement system, (2) The multiparty system, or (3) any other "democratic and representative political system". Then according to Article 99 of the constitution, "During the last month of the fourth year of the term, a referendum shall be held to determine the political system the people of Uganda choose to adopt."

Museveni himself was obviously pleased with the decision of the Assembly. Clearly he saw the avenue opening for him to continue his economic recovery plan free of sectarian politics. While he scorned the tribalism which divided his country, he had particular abhorrence for the religious divisions that the parties capitalized on. To this issue he stated, " There is peace and harmony in the villages. People are no longer at each other's throats over this Catholic and Protestant business." (19) The Prime Minister Kintu Musoke also linked parties to religious divisions as he stated, " Political Parties would lead to a resumptions of unprincipled religious and ethnic sectarianism unacceptable within the concept of national interest in a modern Uganda." (20) Thus the movement to call a halt to political parties was also an attempt to reconstitute the political structures on grounds other than religion. Finally the constitution was promulgated late in 1995 and an Electoral Commission was established so as to plan for and schedule elections by the middle of 1996.

United States Government Response To The Constitution

While there was this internal political discussion about the constitution, the international community was relatively quiet. However, in the later stages of Constituent Assembly action, when it was clear that there would be no multi party system for at least five years, the international community began to question the path Uganda was about to take. On May 12, 1995 the United States Information Service in Kampala released a statement that raised serious objections to the decisions made in the Constituent Assembly. That statement read, " Despite the remarkable progress that Uganda has achieved, The United States now notes with concern that the stage is being set for the entrenchment of a system of government which falls seriously short of full democracy and political enfranchisement.

Some forces would like to see a constitution that preserves monopoly power indefinitely and continues the prohibition on the right of association and the right of assembly. The history of Uganda, like the history of other countries, shows the undesirable, often tragic consequences of governments which do not allow political competition." (21) This statement sent shock waves throughout Kampala and much discussion ensued among the US, other countries monitoring the process, and the Ugandan government itself. The United States did not back down from the statement. Deputy Ambassador Wayne Bush said, "'Article 269 (In the final document the article which restricted parties) restricts genuine political party activity and is a blot on the face of this constitution." (22)

On another occasion he stated, " The new constitution of Uganda does not live up to the promise. Despite some diligent efforts by some Constituent Assembly Delegates, the constitution nevertheless contains serious flaws." (23) He later indicated the US might not help to fund the presidential and parliamentary elections as promised, "The American people will not countenance American government support for an election process that is seriously flawed." (24) The government of Uganda was quick to respond. Vice President Specioza Kazibwe said somewhat sharply that she would, "like to give the US some lessons on No Party Democracy." (25) In another forum she was even more biting, " Whereas our ambassador cannot direct John Major to solve the issue of Catholics in Ireland or Bill Clinton the brutality done to American Negroes, our friends here give us directives."(26)

The Deputy Premier of Uganda said that the "US should not dictate what political system Uganda should have. Instead the US should learn to support African leadership which wants to solve African problems." (27) The National newspaper also responded in editorial fashion. In one editorial it stated the issue quite clearly, " If the meaning of democracy means accommodation of different political ideas by discussion before a consensus is reached, then we have democracy. In the early 1960's Uganda was born with political pluralism. It did not help; it divided the country and led to hatred and killings. Ugandans have not completely discarded political parties but we think it is too early to bring them back after all the problems we have had with parties. What we have now is the democracy we would like to have; we need some time to mature in politics. What we have put in place did come out of the air.

We have developed the movement after considering all the woes parties have caused to our country." (28) A later, even more pointed editorial to the US, stated, " Has it occurred to this giant US that by insisting that democracy is only so if it squares with their own theories, they make themselves less credible? Are the Americans so beholden to their idea of democracy that they are blind to the practical steps a country like Uganda is undertaking to produce a better deal for its citizens?" (29) The President himself also responded to Mr. Bush and the American intervention. He spoke in no uncertain terms, " What the people of Uganda decide is what course we shall take. It is not for the Americans to decide for Ugandans what is best for them. The only point the Americans can make is to insist the parties have equal opportunity to campaign along with the NRM in a referendum to decide their fate before the next elections in the year 2000." (30)

With regard to Mr. Bush's implied threat that the US might not help fund the elections, Museveni replied, " The American ambassador, like any other foreigner, is free to give his views on our politics. But to think that they can force us to change something that has been agreed upon democratically is totally out of the question. Uganda will pay for the elections whether our friends give us aid or not." (31) The US Ambassador Michael Southwick initially was as strong as Mr. Bush. Defending their intervention he stated, " No party democracy is just a reinvention of the discarded one party state.

The US had hoped that Uganda would move less ambiguously toward full democratization. Article 269 (limiting parties) restricts political party activity and is a blot on the face of this constitution." (32) Referring to Museveni's contention that the five year extension was decided democratically, Southwick countered it was the "tyranny of the majority." However strong his statements in defending the US intervention, Southwick was clear not to isolate Museveni stating, " My opinion is that except for Mandela, Museveni stands out at the top of the hill of African leaders." Adding to reporters, " We are trying to avoid a clash of opinion between ourselves and this government." (33) Indeed, when Museveni went to the United Nations late in 1995, indications are that the US tried to temper the rift a bit. Southwick went to Entebbe airport for a private meeting with Museveni before Museveni's departure and in the United States Museveni met with US Secretary of State Christopher. Christopher made no public statement about the constitution, rather commended Uganda for its enormous economic progress.

Finally, Southwick denied rumors that the US might "punish" Uganda by limiting its foreign assistance package saying," The democratic concerns of Uganda should be addressed by Ugandans, in their own fashion and in their own tempo. To link democratization with aid trivializes the issue. However, this should be the final election of this type. If you accept the premise of a no party election, this election doesn't look so bad. But that is if you accept that premise. But we are convinced that Uganda will come up with solutions that look to the future rather than the past." (34)

The 1996 Presidential Elections

Once the constitution was approved the electoral commission began the process of preparing for elections. In an astounding move, the two opposition parties, long bitter rivals, agreed to a coalition for the purposes of a united ticket behind one candidate for president, Paul Ssemogerere, who was a former minister in Museveni's government. What was amazing is that Ssemogerere, a Catholic and a leading member of the DP, was able to unite forces with the rival UPC which was still chaired by Obote in exile in Zambia. Ssemogerere was the DP candidate for President in 1980 when it was rather clear the election was stolen and Obote of the UPC was declared the winner. Now he was combining forces with the very ones that were his sworn enemies just some years previously. Ssemogerere, however, was a wise choice for a unified opposition candidate. He is a Catholic, a Muganda (from Buganda), and a very well respected politician. Many however had difficulty figuring out how these two opposing parties could unite.

In a somewhat satirical editorial the government paper stated, " The country is relieved to know that the old tactics of using tribes and religion to form hatred and confusion in the villages will not apply this time. Since the two parties will field a joint candidate, the prospect of using religion as a platform is about over. Preaching tribal and religious hatred will not work this time." (35) Yet the fears of religious divisions that would disrupt the election never subsided and all parties were sensitive to religious groups becoming too forceful. Early on in the campaign Museveni appealed to religious leaders "not to be tempted to use religion to divide people as the election approaches." (36) Because Ssemogerere is a Catholic and because the Catholic community has felt politically marginalized, there was question as to how the Catholic community might respond in this election. The official statement from the Catholic Cardinal's office in Kampala indicated the church had every intention of staying away from partisan politics. The Cardinal's secretary stated, " The Catholic Church will not throw its weight behind any candidate during the forthcoming elections. Reports that the Church is backing Ssemogerere were bound to come due to past politics. Some are bound to think that since Ssemogerere is a Catholic, then Catholics support him.

But the Catholic church has not taken any position on the issue of movement vs. multiparty. The church is only interested in good leadership and democracy." (37) Responded the national newspaper in an editorial, " Uganda has suffered too much from religious conflict imported from abroad. Imperialists rivalries of the 19th century created religious divisions that persist up to this day and which contributed substantially to the prolonged political crisis of the post independence period. It is good that the Church of Uganda and the Catholic Church have come out strongly to insist that the clergy should not attempt to influence the course of the elections. The people shouldn't get caught in religious sectarianism which is a corruption of religion for selfish political ends." (38)

A controversy arose when a very strident statement was made by a Kampala priest on Easter Sunday, a month away from the election. Rev. Henry Mukasa , carrying a copy of *The New Vision,* told his congregation not to vote for Museveni accusing the NRM of bribing voters. He stated, "It is our money that they are using to buy you. Museveni should stop seeking political capital through his telling of lies." He also accused 2 NRM officials (unnamed) of approaching him trying to bribe him to speak in favor of the NRM. (39)   This story was reported by the non government owned paper, *The Monitor.* Though the *Monitor* had been critical of Museveni, it did not accept the strategy of the priest. On the same day it reported the story, it editorialized, " Priests are beginning to openly take sides in the presidential elections and some are urging worshippers which candidate to vote for. However, partisan politics is a road littered with banana peels for the churches. There are still many problems in Uganda's politics today particularly the violence against opposition candidates and the restrictions on multi parties. These are things the church has a right to raise as issues. In the process, however, the Church cannot seem like an opposition party, or a wing of the NRM. Style is all very important." (40) The regional and rather objective newspaper, *The East African,* sounded a similar theme, "It is with some alarm that in Uganda we observe what looks like the drafting of clergy into camps for the elections. The problem in Rwanda was that the Church was much too closely tied to the government. The involving of Church leaders in political campaigns is hurting the church by killing the authoritative alternative they have exercised in a country where the institutions of democracy and accountability are still young and fragile." (41)

Some few days after all this discussion, the President was campaigning and tried once more to de escalate religious, sectarian sentiment.

Campaigning in a heavily Catholic area likely to support the Catholic Ssemogerere, Museveni stated, " I am willing to accept a Catholic president for Uganda but not a weak one like Ssemogerere. There are people saying ' Let Catholics rule'. I have no objection, but I have to see first if that person is capable. Not Ssemogerere; he was weak and just looked on when our people were being killed. There is no problem if the President is Catholic or Muslim, but he must be strong." (42) . On May 5, 1996, four days before election day, I had the opportunity to have a personal interview with President Museveni. I had been trying for months to see him, working every contact I could. I finally got notice that I could see him at his mountain retreat in Fort Portal, at the other end of the country where I have been living in Jinja.

It clearly wasn't going to be easy to get there, a full day journey by public vans. But I made the trip, attended his campaign rally and then was escorted to his retreat. The interview with the President touched on several themes of this chapter. I discussed with him Julius Nyerere's praise of his movement system and asked him if he thought the model of democracy he has developed in Africa could serve other developing countries who had undergone similar years of political upheaval like Uganda. His first point to this question was to insist that though he firmly believes in the movement system, he is not opposed to parties in principle. He contends that Uganda is "politically immature at this point" and to have parties now is to "ask for trouble."

More to the question he interestingly responded, "I am not in the business of prosletyzing my theory of democracy to all of Africa. However, I do think it could be applicable in certain countries. But I am concentrating my efforts on convincing the citizens of Uganda about the merits of this system." He also insisted that the movement is a critical stage in "the democratization process." Though he is philosophically tied to the Movement at this point, he claims to see an evolution of democracy in Uganda. He said that in the referendum to be held in four years, if the people ask for a return to the party system, he will comply. (43)

Of course, there are many who fear that he is posturing and that he has no intentions of bowing to the will of the people should they vote for a return to parties. We spoke of the United States interventions of Summer of 1995 which were extremely critical of the NRM and the present electoral process. I indicated that the US seemed to soften its stance of late and asked him if that were indeed the case. He stated that it was accurate to say the US position was less strident now. He attributed that to his visit to the UN in the fall of 1995 when he met with Warren Christopher and officials at the State Department who seemed to give him a different signal than the US ambassador in Kampala was. Clearly he seemed to be saying the US was taking one public opinion through the ambassador but was quietly giving him another position more supportive of his implementation of Movement democracy. (44)

I also explored President Museveni's thoughts on the role of religion in present day Ugandan politics. Obviously in the past he has been quite critical of the role of religion as an institution that gave impetus to sectarian divisions based on tribal and religious grounds. These socio - religious divisions helped to give birth to the political parties which continued to follow the same sectarian separations. I asked him if he thought the problem were as bad as it had been or was there evidence that such religious differences were playing less a role in dividing society politically. Again, he prefaced his answer before he responded directly. He explained his philosophy of development that he hopes will promote a greater cohesiveness within Ugandan society. He said political divisions in Western industrial societies are very often based on economic interest, horizontally cutting across ethnic and religious divisions.

However, in Uganda, the divisions are more vertically defined, based on tribe and religion. The critical problem in his eyes is the fact there is no real middle class with common economic interests in Uganda. Thus there is no economic or political interest that might overcome the religious and tribal divisions. One of the political benefits of his enormous economic progress is that he is slowly building up a solid business, middle class in addition to a more organized labor force and working class. It is his firm hope that these economic interests will connect people from various tribes and religions.

Thus economic interests provide the horizontal leverage that begins to break down the vertical barriers. These economic interests could lead to a reconfiguration of the political parties, focusing not on tribal or religious interests, rather on economic goals. More specifically to the question, he stated that it is true that , on the whole, organize religion has been less divisive in this election. However, he did express two reservations. He said he had meetings with religious leaders to try to develop a "Code of Conduct" that would guide religious and political leaders at a time of election. He was unsuccessful in that effort and indicated he will continue such efforts before the next elections to be held in five years.

He also expressed disappointment with "that priest in Kampala", meaning no doubt the parish priest who publically condemned him on Easter Sunday. However, he seemed more annoyed than concerned and thought that overall the "picture is improving." I have the distinct impression that he attributes the improvement more to his economic progress and the horizontal - vertical analogy than to improvement in the religious climate. (45) On election day, Museveni won an overwhelming victory. 73% of the electorate turned out to vote and Museveni won 32 out of the 39 districts, losing only in the North where the Kony rebels are quite active. Nationwide, he won 74.2% of the 6,163,678 votes cast. Paul Ssemogerere, the multipartyist candidate received 23.7% of the vote and Mohammed Mayanja, an independent, won 2.1% of the vote. The election process was very peaceful with only scattered charges of voter irregularity.

Though Ssemogerere called the election rigged, teams of international observers numbering several hundred, called the election process quite fair. Interestingly enough, the Catholic Cardinal of Kampala was generous in his praise of Museveni as he stated, " The news of your landslide victory in the first national elections of this Republic is, in all corners greeted with great joy. On behalf of the Catholic church in Uganda, allow me to offer congratulations. During the last decade of your leadership of Uganda we have experienced great recovery, progress, and growth in various aspects of our lives. I trust that we will experience even more in the years to come." (46)

When the final tabulation was announced on national radio, I was struck by the spontaneous celebrations that occurred in our village. I quickly took a bicycle ride around the area and there was much jubilation. People were out on the roads singing, marching in spontaneous parades, drinking and celebrating. It seemed clear to me at the grass roots level, the people were relieved and quite satisfied that there would be no change of government. The spontaneous celebrations seemed to give an authenticity to the voting. Museveni's argument that five more years of economic progress and relative peace is more important than a return to multi parties seemed to strike a deep cord in the minds of the average Ugandan. The philosophical argument of style of democracy raised by the US and other Western powers was less important to these celebrating Ugandans than economic and peace issues.

The Ugandan Experiment - A Model Of Democracy ?

Yoweri Museveni has developed a model of democracy that has not received universal approval. As I have documented, foreign governments, particularly the United States, raised serious objections. Internal political opposition protested the lack of multiparities. Church leaders questioned the even handedness of the electoral process. Yet through it all Museveni has insisted that his model of democracy is correct for Uganda at this time in its history. Considering the violent past of partisan Ugandan politics, the reign of terrors conducted by the Amin and Obote regimes, the Civil War, the sectarian tribal divisions fueled by religious differences, Museveni contends that his model which stresses unity and aims for economic progress is the only suitable one for Uganda at this point. He points to the nationwide elections to the Constituent Assembly, the grass roots consultation on the constitution, and local governing bodies as proof that he has taken democracy seriously. He simply feels Uganda is not yet ready for a more open multiparty model of democracy, a model that could once again open sectarian divisions that nearly destroyed the country.

Julius Nyerere, one of the elder statesmen of African politics seems to concur with Museveni. He states, " Democracy is not a commodity that can be lifted from a shelf and given life. A nation can draw ideas and learn from elsewhere but only the very foolish or very arrogant believe that there exists a template for a perfect prototype of democracy which has only to be produced for democracy to flourish. Forms of truly democratic organization will differ from country to country. The mechanisms of democracy are not the meaning of democracy. They are only the means to an end.

Democracy means that people must be able to choose freely those who govern them and that the government must be accountable to them, responsive to views expressed freely through a political machinery which the people can understand and use. They will understand and use it if the machinery makes sense in their own culture. The forms of democracy, and the machinery of democracy, now operative in the countries of Europe and North America have evolved and been developed over many centuries, and it is these powerful and developed countries which now presume to judge the democracy of young states in Africa. President Yoweri Museveni remains unimpressed by those who blame tribalism or religious bigotry for the sins of bankrupt politicians. I believe that under his leadership Uganda has a better chance for national development than she ever had since independence." (47). A Ugandan professor in London echoed a similar theme," Uganda has adopted the underlying universal principles of democracy - popular participation, free and fair elections, freedom of expression, freedom of the press, accountability of government, and independence of a judiciary.

The principles are there; how they are implemented may vary from nation to nation." (48) And Museveni himself stated, "It is a mistake to copy Western democracies. Democracies can work in our countries only if the internal forces are allowed to work without manipulation. Democracy must evolve; it cannot be forced or the whole thing could blow apart." (49) And so, on May 9,1996, President Yoweri Museveni was declared for the first time as the elected President of Uganda. His election is perhaps an affirmation of the work he has done in bringing the country out of economic and political chaos to a time of relative prosperity and peace. Whether it is an uncritical affirmation of his political philosophy of a "no party democracy" is a somewhat debatable question. It is clear however, that the voters were willing to go five more years with this man as their president, with the movement as their government. He has promised that in four years time the people will decide on the form of democracy to be taken.

The international community, the DP and the UPC, and the churches await to see if that will be the case. Nyerere stated that each measure of democracy must be developed within the particular societal context. Museveni has developed his style within the Ugandan context. He himself states the Movement is a stage in the "democratization of Uganda". Others fear the Movement is a charade of a stage for democracy but rather a stage for ultimate dictatorship. As a political scientist, as one who has lived in Uganda for two years, as one who has followed closely the political events and who has spoken to the president, I tend to think it is a stage for democracy. However, political life in the developing world in general, Africa in particular, is very unpredictable.

If Museveni continues on the same track of economic progress and also opens up the political system as promised, his movement government may indeed serve as a model for developing counties trying to move to democracy after chaos and violence without adopting a multi party system that may lead back to instability. If on the other hand, he continues with economic progress and fails to do as he promised in opening up the political system, we have sadly witnessed another disappointing moment in the rather painful political history of Uganda.

Notes
1. "Interest Groups and Institution Building Processes in Uganda", Dan Mudoola, Makerere University Press, 1992.
2. *New Vision*, February 6, 1995, p. 9.
3. *New Vision*, March 8, 1996, p.40.
4.."What is Africa's Problem?", Yoweri Museveni, NRM Publications, Kampala, 1992 , p.22.
5. *ibid.*, p.25.
6. *ibid.*, p.33.
7. *The New Vision*, Kampala, January 29, 1995, p. 22.
8. *Foreign Affairs*, "An African Success Story", Bill Berkley, September, 1994,

p.28.

9. *ibid.* p.30.

10. *New Vision,* April 25, 1996, p.15.

11. Museveni, *op.cit.,* p.279.

12. Berkley, *op.cit.,* p.24.

13. *Africa Report,* "No To Multi Party", Catharine Watson, May, 1994, p.24.

14. *New Vision,* May 30, 1995, p.1.

15. *New Vision,* June 22, 1995, p.1.

16. *The East African,* June 19, 1995, p.11.

17. *The Sunday Vision,* June 18, 1995, p.5.

18. *New Vision,* June 23, 1995, p.4.

19. Watson, *op.cit.,* p.25.

20. *New Vision,* March 6, 1996, p.3.

21. USIS Press Release, Kampala, May 12, 1995.

22. *The Monitor,* October 18, 1995, p.1.

23. *New Vision, October* 16, 1995, p. 1..

24. *East African,* October 16, 1995, p. 1.

25. *Monitor,* June 17, 1995, p.1.

26. *New Vision,* February 14, 1996, p.3.

27. *New Vision,* May 16, 1995, p.1.

28. *New Vision,* October 20, 1995, p.5.

29. *New Vision,* October 22, 1995, p.6.

30. *New Vision,* May 19, 1995, p.1.

31. *New Vision* October 16, 1995, p.1.

32. *Monitor,* October 18, 1995, p.1.

33. *ibid.*

34. *East African,* January 15, 1996, p.1.

35. *New Vision,* September 5, 1995, p. 1.

36. *New Vision,* March 4, 1996, p. 40.

37. *New Vision,* march 7, 1996, p.1.

38. *New Vision,* March 15, 1996, p.1.

39. *Monitor,* April 10, 1996, p. 1.

40. *Monitor,* April 10, 1996, p.3.

41. *East African,* December 18, 1995, p.10.

42. *Monitor,* April 24, 1996, p. 1.

43. Personal Interview with President Yoweri Museveni, Presidential Retreat House, Fort Portal, Uganda, May 5, 1996.

44. *ibid.*

45. *ibid.*

46. *New Vision,* May 14, 1996,p.10.

47. Museveni, Yoweri, *op.cit.,* p.12-13.

48. *New Vision,* March 13, 1996, p.7.

49. *New York Times,* June 21, 1994, p.1

Chapter 6

Namibia- Africa's Last Colony: A Democratic Experiment

Bamidele A. Ojo

The on going democratic changes in Africa is a product of the New World Order which has opened up the political space and stem the hemorrhaging and decadent civil society on the continent.

Namibia is a product of this euphoric change. Liberated from the illegal occupation of apartheid South Africa, through a combined liberation struggle led by the South West African Peoples Organization [SWAPO] and the diplomatic maneuvers at the international level by the United Nations, Namibia attained its independence on May 21st. 1990.

The independence was preceded by an election of November 1989 within the context of The UN Resolution 435 but the new country had its first democratic election in November of 1994, thus marking the end of the first stage of democratic institutionalization of Africa's last colony.

The objective in this chapter is to examine the democratic transition in Namibia within the context of the democratization process in Africa while critically analyzing the roles of major actors such as SWAPO, other political parties and the elites therein , in an attempt to identify the prospect for consolidation of democratic ideals and institutions in the Country. Divided into two parts, the first presents an overview of the Namibian democratic transition through to its independence.

An historical overview becomes indispensable as well as the analysis of the electoral politics preceding the independence. The second part examines the ascension to power of the SWAPO government and the first four year of democratic rule culminating in the last election.

Namibia: Geography

Namibia is situated in the South West corner of Africa and covers an area of 824,295 sq kilometers(or 717,827 sq. miles) which is twice the size of California in the United States. To its north is the state of Angola and Botswana to its east. To the northeast is the Caprivi strip which touches Zambia and Zimbabwe. To the south of Namibia is the Republic of South Africa and to its west lies the Atlantic Ocean.This Country can be divided topographically into three regions: the Namib desert, the Central Plateau and the kalahari desert. The Namib desert lies along the South Atlantic coast and stretches along the entire length of the country from the Angolan border to the South African Border. It covers about a fifth of the landscape and barely habitable. However, this part of the country is rich in mineral resources such as diamonds, uranium, salt and its water are one of the best for fishing in the World.

The Namibian central plateau which rises 3,000 to 9,000 feet above sea level covers over half of the total area of the country. It also contains mineral deposits of copper, lead, zinc, tin, vanadium, sulfur, cadmium, silver, lithium, iron, germanium ,uranium and many other precious metals. Its northern part is also suited for grazing.

The kalahari desert lies in the east and north and it is characterized by layers of terrestrial sand and limestone but receives scanty rainfall. Its southern part is suited for grazing by karakul sheep. But its eastern portion is quite arid, barren and lifeless (Kiljunen,M-L,1981:23-25; Moleah,A.T,1983:). With this type of physical landscape, Namibia is prone to prolong drought. And water problems is worsen by the fact that there are only four perennial border rivers: The Kunene, the Okavango and the Zambesi in the north and the Orange in the south.

Namibia: Its People.

Namibia like many other African States, is made up of many ethnic groups. Its diverse population has one of the lowest density in the World, about 0.5 person per kilometers and with a population of about a million and   half, Namibians can be divided into four main groups (Ojo,B.A.,1991):
- the khoisans
- the Bantus
- the Sangmeles
- the Europeans

The Khoisans:

This ethnic group includes the Bushmen, the Damaras and the Namas. The Bushmen(Bouchiman or Sans) are the oldest inhabitant of Namibia [formerly South West Africa]. They are predominantly hunters , gatherers and normads.

The Bantus:

Most of these group came from central Africa's great lake area and they includes: The Ovambos, which could be sub-divided into the Kwanyamas, the kwanbis, the Ngandgeras, the Mbalantus, the Kwalundhis, the Nkolonkathis and the Eundas. Close to the Ovambos are the Kavangos, who are also a diverse group made up of five sub-ethnic groups, which includes the Kwangaris, the Bungas, the Shumbiis, the Djirikus and the Hambukushus. They speak three different languages: Kwangali is spoken in the west of Kavango, the Goiviku in the center and the Mbukushu in the east. Moreover, the family structure of the Kavangos is matrilineal.

The Hereros is another Bantus sub-ethnic group. They came from the Massamedo region in Angola a few centuries after the Ovambos and the Kavangos. And the Hereros are warriors as well. Another group is the Caprivians, made up of the Masubias and the Mafwes are divided into Chiefdoms, at the head of which is the Chief assisted by a prime-Minister or "Ngambele" and also by advisory chiefs. They are mostly farmers and cattle rearers and speaks the Silozi.

The Ovambos, the kavangos, the Hereros and the Caprivians constitute the majority of the Bantus and some of them live along the Namibian border with Botswana.

The Sangmeles:

This group include the Oorlams, the Basters and the coloreds. The Oorlams are hottentots, the descendants of the first group of Europeans from the Cape(South Africa). The Basters are descendants of holland fathers and khoi mothers from the north-west region of the Cape province.

The Coloreds came from South Africa between the two World Wars. And are fishermen who lived along the ports of Walvis Bay, Luderitz , Windhoek and Keetmanshoop.

And the *Europeans* are made up of groups of missionaries and merchants from the north, east and south of Namibia. Many of which are English, Jews(from Angola) and Italians. There are also Germans among this group. Afrikaner member of this group came mostly since the South African Occupation of Namibia.

Historical Overview

The People of the territory now known as Namibia, has until recently [1990] been subjected to one form of colonial administration or the other. First by the Germans starting from the formal establishment of its Protectorate in 1884. And later by the South Africans, with the defeat of the Germans in the First world war in 1915.

Namibia in its earliest history experienced bloody wars arising from ; internal communal conflict before and during German occupation; resistance against the Germans, which led to repression of genocidal proportion of the Hereros and the Namas especially between 1904 and 1908 , during which about 75% of these ethnic groups perished (Ojo,B.A.,1989).

The entire African population in this territory, then known as South West Africa lost their lands and means of subsistence and became subject of discriminatory laws. The situation became worse with the introduction of the pass laws and the enforcement of contract labor- a source of cheap labor which became so productive for the colonial administration that series of laws were promulgated to facilitate the continuation of the system. For example, the Native regulation act was passed in 1907 because of the need for more labor. This turn the north into a source of cheap and exploited labor and later led to the introduction of the migrant labor system.

This system lasted until the 1970s but it brought in its wake, increased national awareness which led to the formation of nationalist movements, which will eventually put an end to the system and the entire structure of apartheid. Namibia was entrusted in 1920 to the South African government on behalf of the British, under the system of Mandate C of the League of Nations. With the coming to power of the Nationalist Party in the Union of South Africa in 1948 and the introduction of apartheid policy in the territory, the administration of Namibia contradicted the terms and the spirit of the trust as expressed in the mandate of the League of Nations- because of the exploitation of the people and resources of the country to the benefits of only the minority whites.

The administrative activities of South Africa in Namibia was characterized by :

1). The exploitation of the natural resources of the territory, with the help of cheap indigenous labor and 2). Acquisition of farmlands for white

South Africans. This was part of a deliberate effort to incorporate Namibia into the Union, which was met with international protest.

Within Namibia itself, the discriminatory and exploitative nature of the administration was met with outright resistance which in turn led to repressive actions and continued subjugation of the African population, i.e. the Mandume revolt in 1917, the Bondelzwarts in 1922, the Rehoboth Basters in 1925 and the Impumbu revolt of 1932.

Despite resistance by the people of Namibia, the South African government also went ahead with its apartheid policy of 'homelands' for eleven African ethnic groups - which further aggravated the political situation and energized nationalist resistance. For example, the United Nations demanded the withdrawal of the South African government from Namibia in 1957 because of conflicts with provisions of the mandate and its charter.

The Namibia question became from there on an international problem which was considered a threat to the peace and security of the world. Domestic resistance was initially established as a protest front against apartheid policies and to campaign for international support against racist South Africa. Prominent among these movements is the Ovambo People's Organization(OPO), which was established in 1957 under the leadership of Adimba Toivo ya Toivo and Sam Nujoma, to protest against the migrant labor system. Another movement established during the same period was the South West African National Union(SWANU).

Some of these movements extended their range of objectives to include national liberation , full participation in the affairs of the state and independence. These changes was a product of both the waves of decolonization across the continent and the continued brutal and repressive responses of the South African Government. The Windhoek Massacre of 1959, for example, forced many of the leaders of these organizations underground and into exile(The Ovambo People's Organization became the South West African People's Organization(SWAPO), which had both its internal and external wings working simultaneously against the racist regime).

SWAPO's influence increased with its continued activities outside the country, which could be attributed to the pragmatic approach of its leadership and organization. This enabled it to receive the support of the Organization of African Unity(OAU) and eventually the recognition of the United Nations in 1973, as the authentic representative of the Namibian People. With the 1966 decision of the International Court of Justice, in a case brought before it by Liberia and Ethiopia on the illegality of the South

Contemporary African Politics:

African occupation of Namibia, SWAPO decided to launch its next phase of the resistance, by complementing its political initiatives with military activities , parallel to the initiative s of the United Nations. The first armed conflict between the two forces(SWAPO and South Africa) took place at Ongulumbashe on the 26th of August 1966.

International focus on Namibia was intensified with the establishment of a UN Council for Namibia(1967) and the declaration of the UN Security Council on December 16 1968, that the presence of South Africa in the territory was illegal. SWAPO became the symbol of Namibia national resistance and in a series of Congresses and declarations emphasized its commitment to the unity of Namibian people in order to safeguard its(Namibia) independence. SWAPO received financial and material assistance from many countries and international organizations and mostly from the Eastern bloc.

Given the dynamics of the East-West rivalry during this period, SWAPO became associated with socialist movements. Its doctrinal predisposition which was no less than an appropriate vehicle to mobilize against an imperialist and racist occupying foreign domination, was used as a reason for preserving South African rule and in delaying UN resolutions on Namibia. Through the diplomatic efforts of the Contact Group (five western members of the UN Security Council-the United States, Britain, Germany, France and Canada) and the adoption of the UNSC resolution 435 in 1978, a turning point in the decolonization of Namibia was reached and it reaffirmed the legal responsibility of the United Nations over the country - with emphasis on a UN supervised transition to independence.

The South African government resisted any attempt at implementing the resolution and with the support of its allies in the UN Security council, the Namibian problem continued until 1990. South Africa initiated an internal settlement involving anti-SWAPO organizations but it failed because of lack of International support. With the support of the United States, the support for the implementation, in a series of diplomatic efforts was linked to the withdrawal of Cuban forces from Angola. Other factors influencing the dramatic change also included the changing world order wherein communism became less of a threat to the West; the failure of the transitional government created by South Africa to pre-empt Resolution 435; the growing financial difficulties resulting from UN sanctions on South Africa and the continue pressure against the war in Namibia, which was becoming more like South Africa's Vietnam (especially after South Africa suffered a terrible defeats at Cuito Cuanavale in early 1988, in the hands of SWAPO combatants(PLAN),

Angolans and Cubans).

The final tripartite agreement was signed on December 22 1988, in New York between Angola, Cuba and South Africa, with the United States and Soviet Union as observers and it paved the way for the final implementation of Resolution 435.

Resolution 435 And Independence.

Resolution 435 was a decision of the United Nations Security Council affirming a UN proposal for settlement in Namibia. Compiled by the five western countries [Contact Group], the resolution was a Peace Plan negotiated with all parties concerned(South Africa, the frontline states, SWAPO and other parties within Namibia). It was based on Internationally accepted democratic principles which provided for a free and fair elections that will elect members of a constituent assembly which will write up a Constitution that will be approved by two-third of its membership.

The resolution provided for a constitution guaranteeing a bill of fundamental human rights, including the right to freedom of speech, movement, private ownership of property and a Government under law of the constitution. And that the constitution should also guarantee an independent judiciary and regular democratic elections. The resolution also provided for the use of proportional representation in the election into the constituent assembly. Voting during the election was for parties which in turn will be represented in the assembly according to the percentage of votes received. The resolution also provided for an international transitional assistance force(the UN Transition Assistance Group-UNTA) composed to the maximum satisfaction of all the parties. The transitional assistance force will monitor the implementation of the resolution and ensure free and fair election.

The resolution also provided, for an orderly disengagement and withdrawal of the troops of the warring parties and assistance to returnees and the release of political prisoners. It also gave the Administrator-General the supervisory power over the election. His administration was to monitor the UNTAG in order to ensure impartiality. The resolution in addition to the aforementioned, demanded for the abolition of all discriminatory laws and the maintenance of laws and order during the transitional period preceding independence.

It must be emphasized that the UNSC resolution 435 of 1978 was complemented by a lot of other resolutions and agreements which when read together provided for the constitutional principles of independent Namibia. The agreement of 1982, for example, detailed the basis of democracy during the transitional period:

Section A of the agreement covers the procedures and principles that governed the election for the Constituent Assembly and the decision making process therein. Section B described the basic principles which was included in the Constitution such as Namibia must be a unitary, sovereign and   democratic state. It also included declarations of fundamental human rights consistent with the Universal Declaration of Human Rights.

Another important document relevant to the resolution
was the final implementation of the decision of the Resolution 632 of February 16 1989, which made specific reference to the composition and functions of UNTAG. For example, the UN Secretary-General in this document emphasized the impartial role of the United Nations, the start of the implementation of Resolution 435-April 1st. 1989 and monitoring of SWAPO bases by UNTAG(UNSC S/15287/July 12 1982). UNTAG was important component of the entire process. It was responsible to and under the control of the UN Security Council. It consisted of the following:

The Special Representative of the UN Secretary-General

The Election monitoring Unit of over 1000 members

The military unit under a Commander which was made up of over 4000 members.

The Police Adviser unit of about 500

 The UN High Commission for Refugees and its staff (which assisted and helped to resettle Returnees).

The Chief Administrative Officer and his Staff.

The Implementation started with a hitch, whereby conflict broke out between SWAPO and South African forces leaving over 300 dead, this was as a result of a misinterpretation of the part of the Peace Plan dealing with SWAPO combatants(an analysis of this incident can be found in Ojo,B.A.'s, Namibia, SWAPO, and International Politics: The Politics of Decolonization and National Liberation In a New World Environment, forthcoming in the spring of 1999).

The Transition

After the initial problem concerning the conflict between SWAPO and South African forces , the implementation went as scheduled. A total of 701269 Namibians registered to vote and given the diversity of the population there were many of political parties representing different ethnic and ideological groups and in many cases reflecting their positions during the liberation struggle.The platforms of the different Political Parties reflected constitutional preferences and their plans for a future Namibia. For Example:

The *Aksie Christelik Nasional(ACN)* envisioned the protection of group rights and the respect of language rights while recognizing Agriculture, Mining and fisheries as the industrial base for a stable and material welfare of Namibia.

The *Christian Democratic Action for Social Justice (CDA)* was for a strong central government.

The *Democratic Turnhalle Alliance(DTA)* guarantees fundamental rights and support the total removal of pre independent governmental structures.

The *Federal Convention of Namibia(FCN)* declared its commitment to respect fundamental human rights of Namibians to own private land and to maintain link with other groups and to facilitate expansion with respect to communication, transportation ,etc.

The *Namibian National Democratic Party(NNDP)* emphasized social welfare and an economic policy capable of providing sufficient credit facilities, technical help and education.

The *Namibian National Front (NNF)* was for a unicameral legislature with an Executive President and also the provision of free and comprehensive national health service.

The *National Patriotic Front of Namibia(NPF)* identified with the supremacy of the law and the creation of jobs and protection against deprivation.

The *SWAPO-Democrats(SWAPO-D)*. These are former members of SWAPO who in some cases still share the same values as their former Organization. This party envisioned a multi- party democracy and the provision of social security, equal and compulsory education for all, up to the age of Sixteen.

The *South West African Peoples Organization(SWAPO)* in its own platform emphasized a preference for a unitary, secular and democratic state in which there is Social justice. It also supports the use of English as the national language.

The *United Democratic Front of Namibia(UDF)* supported a democratic and stable multi-party State. It also envisioned a State that guarantees fundamental rights.

It must be emphasized that these parties are in most cases composed of political parties in alliance in order to be able to win the election. And from the brief identification of the general themes of their platform, some basic aspirations predominates. Among them are fundamental human rights, a multi- party democracy, a guarantee of education and health care and the use of English as a national language.

The reason for the emphases on these themes is a function of not only was the electoral process under the United Nations supervision but that the resolution under which these Parties were contesting the election presupposed many of these principles. More so, this is a country that has been under foreign domination , in which its majority has been exploited under a racist regime and had experienced extensive national liberation war. More importantly, there is a preexisting values among these people that went beyond the coming of the Europeans. The parties are also cognizance of the influence and the international support that the SWAPO had and that many of them had worked with the South Africa within the country while the war was going on. There is also the Ovambo factor and its potential dominance of the Namibian politics.

     With the possibility of a SWAPO government and given its leftist orientations while taking cognizance of earlier examples in Zimbabwe, Angola and Mozambique, these Parties were very much aware of the fact that a One-Party State is possible. An option which the SWAPO said it would consider only if the people wanted it-through a referendum. But the most important and uniting factor is the fact that all the parties campaigned for independence.

     It was obvious from the onset that voting was not going to be based on issues but on political parties and their ethnic base. Namibians voted between November 8 and 11 of 1989 and elected 72 members of the Constituent Assemble.

The Election of November 8 1989.

     High electoral participation of 95.65% was experienced at the first democratic election in Namibia, in fact only 1.4% of the 670830 votes cast were declared null.

     The DTA led by Dirk Mudge led all the other parties after results from twenty-two of the twenty-three electoral districts were declared but the last district- Ovamboland represented over 35% of the votes.The 212505 votes of the Ovamboland represented 92,03% of the total votes received by the SWAPO (Bulletin quotidien del'AFP,Nov. 18,1989). SWAPO came first in only nine of the twenty-three national polling districts, which reinforced the fact that its is an Ovambo Party. In fact, if electoral results from ovamboland and the districts with large numbers of Ovambo voters(such as Tsumeb, Windhoek, Swakopmund and Luderit) were ignored, its average support would be about 25.8%. Moreover, SWAPO had between 10 and 14.4% in ethnic areas such as Kaokoland and Hereroland.

However, SWAPO led all the other parties with 41 seats of which all the other ethnic groups were represented including four Whites, two colored, and a Baster. Among the four whites was a lawyer, a farmer from the South, a lecturer in bible studies and an housewife. Three of the four women elected into the Assembly were SWAPO members and the other was a DTA member. In Damaraland, SWAPO received two times less vote than the United Democratic front(UDF) which was a Damara Party. It was defeated in the Rehoboth region(about ninty kilometers south of Windhoek) the homeland of the Basters.

The DTA received 28.55% of the votes cast but it must be noted that, inspite of the fact that the DTA is a made up of multi-racial and conservative alliances and that many of the whites voted for it, only two of its representatives were white(in fact of the 72 elected representatives, 9 were whites).

The electoral results reaffirmed the ethnic diversity of the Namibia population. With exception of the colored and the whites, the family remains the center of socio-economic activities in Namibia. The groups that you belong to still takes precedence over the individual thereby reinforcing a communal orientation very much common in African societies.

Just as with other intra and inter ethnic relationships, the Namibian ethnic groups also have different perceptions of each other that is deeply rooted in their history. For example, the Damaras used to be slaves to the Hereros, the Hereros and the Namas and the Hereros and the Ovambos are long time enemies. This was why many of the other ethnic groups feared a SWAPO or an Ovambo domination.

From the foregoing*:

> The Ovambos voted for SWAPO.
>
> The Damaras voted for UDF and DTA.
>
> The Hereros, the Namas and Whites voted for DTA.
>
> The Whites also voted for the ACN
>
> The Basters voted for FCN.

Given the afore mentioned observations, it was apparent that years of liberation struggle had not broken the pervasive ethnic cleavages that existed in the Country. However, Hidipo Hamutenya, a former SWAPO Secretary of Information and Publicity and the Namibian Minister for Information, said in an interview, immediately after the election, that "no Political Party can expect to win power without winning half of the votes from the North"(Ojo,B.A.,1991).

From the onset, it was obvious that the SWAPO would need to work with other parties in order to impose any of its principles on the constituent Assembly. But the desire for reconciliation led to a more cooperative attitude among the representatives. The constitution was approved by a consensus of all parties. In it are provision for a mixed economy and the respect for human rights. It also envisaged an equal economic development for all part of the country. The constitution also provided for an executive president and a two chamber legislature.

Following the adoption of a constitution and the inauguration of an independent Namibia under President Sam Nujoma, past SWAPO activities against its dissident resurfaced and it had negative effects on the new administration efforts at national reconciliation especially among the Namas and Damaras.

It is also important to emphasized the role of the United Nations in the transition of Namibia to statehood, which is a unique diplomatic engagement. It was the first of its kind and many questioned the impartiality of the UN because of the close relationship it had entertain with the SWAPO for many years. It must also be said that it is almost impossible for any Party to win an election in Namibia without the considerable support of the Ovambos, who incidentally were the most affected by the guerrilla war carried out by SWAPO, in the northern part of the country.

The SWAPO Government And The Search For Democratic Institutionalization And Development

On the March 21 1990, Namibia became independent and the 160th member of the United Nations. The UN thus attained another level of excellence in its decolonization activities. This added a new dimension to international law and the extent of the effect of UN and its resolutions on sovereign member states. The new world order has turned the UN into the most viable option in inter state relationship and provides the theater for conflict resolution, peace-making and peace enforcement. Not only has the Namibian independence reinforced this but the gulf war and other international engagements of the organization continue to add to its new roles.

The new SWAPO government emphasized its desire for democracy and development within the framework of national reconciliation. The government's desire for joint ventures involving local, private and foreign capital and the government as the main stay of the economy, was a major shift in the doctrinal predisposition of SWAPO whose main ideological orientation for many years was public ownership of the means of production and the nationalization of the public sector.

The policy change was described as a desire to reach a meeting point with other sections of the Society without eliminating anyone in the spirit of national reconciliation and national unity. The question was the ability of the new government to readapt and restructure itself from a movement of national liberation to a legitimate and democratically elected representative of the people.

Not only did the SWAPO government inherited a budgetary deficit of over $750 million, which placed restrictions on job creation and strains on imports but it faced a very high expectation of socio-political and economic upliftment from the people. The government therefore had to depend on foreign aid and resurgence of foreign investment. In its search for development therefore, the SWAPO administration believed the consolidation of the Namibian economy within a democratic framework guaranteed by the Constitution is an indispensable vehicle towards meeting the aspirations of its people.

Development seen as a process of progressive change plus growth from which a whole society could equally benefits, the government aimed to provide something better for its people [an improvement on the past] such as in education, income, coupled with social equity and justice. It was apparent that these progress will have to be overtime which requires the willingness on the part of the people to accept and work hard for desirable changes, necessary effective social, economic and physical planning in order to stimulate changes and guide them in the right directions.

The past four years of the SWAPO government indicated the readiness of the State and the SWAPO government to" create effective political and economic management capable of ensuring that available natural resources, capital, manpower and technology are all combined efficiently in the process of production" (Oyugi & Gitonga,1987:150-162). This is demonstrated by its adherence to constitutional framework without following in the path of other liberation movement turned government like in Zimbabwe, Mozambique or Angola. Considering the complex nature of these processes, especially in relation to the international economic structure , the dominant western influences on the socio-political and economic infrastructures, the economic attachment to South Africa(a product of the years of occupation) and the control of South Africa over Walvis Bay(which was relinquished a few years back)-Namibia's best port, it will take political and economic stability on the long run for these progress to be visible.

Moreover, the characteristics of the Namibian economy makes short work of the government's efforts. The following characteristics has and will continue to make economic development difficult:
~low agricultural productivity
~low level of average income with a large section of
the society with no income at all
~high incident of illiteracy and general ignorance
~low life expectancy of birth and high infant
mortality rate
~wide spread social despondency
~scarcity of resources and
~low level of industrialization (Totemeyer,1989).
Most of these are a product of either the communal nature of the society, the apartheid and racial policies of the outgone occupying powers or the geographical situation of the country.

Conclusions

SWAPO enjoyed majority in parliament through out the first four years and won a landslide victory in the local and regional elections as well. In Namibia , peace reign and every body enjoys freedom of speech and democracy, which many characterized as "collector items in Africa"(Africa Report,Nov.-Dec.'94)
After the UN control election which brought SWAPO to power, the opposition was expected to be more organized in time for the first democratic election in independent Namibia but the contrary was the case.The main opposition party, the DTA led by Mishake Muyongo has lost most of its credibility because of many reasons which includes, its history of collaboration with Pretoria during the South African attempted interim solution, in an attempt to sidestep the UN Resolution.
The Party is neither universal, for example, outside the Caprivi strip and in some part of Hereroland, the DTA cannot boast of any strong followership. There are even fewer young leaders emerging to rekindle the party. Dirk Mudge has since retired and Mishake Muyongo charisma has since lost its power. When the newly created Democratic Coalition for Namibia [DCN] was formed many observers thought it may be a credible opposition to SWAPO because of the prevailing anti-SWAPO votes that could easily be tapped. However, the inability of the opposition to effectively organize against SWAPO and coupled with the ambitions of the opposition leaders, these parties has in themselves been the architect of the SWAPO dominance.

Within SWAPO itself, ambitions has been checked because of the belief in Sam Nujoma as the winning ticket. Nujoma continue to control the party and this was reinforced in the November 1994 election, when he personally handpicked the top 32 of the party's 72 candidates on the electoral list, without consultation with the grassroot members of the party. These 32 were no doubt guaranteed a seat in parliament and government. The rest of the list was selected by the party at a special electoral college.

Considering the fact that SWAPO was guaranteed between 40 and 50 seats out of the 72, President Nujoma surely pulls the string. In a way SWAPO as a party remain united and in control.

The first four years was not that exemplary. The unemployment rate was high, wealth distribution was not taken seriously , corruption was and remain rampant and plans for Walvis bay remain largely unimplemented. And SWAPO continue to be seen as the liberator. The SWAPO (as a party),the government and Namibia remain synonymous. It is difficult to be anti SWAPO without being unpatriotic and ironically, the absence of strong opposition seems to have kept the party together and one could only hope may be that would probably   make it(the government) more accountable.

As it won the November 1994 election with a landslide majority, there was the fear that, if it acquires the two-third majority, which is 48, it might use its dominance to change the constitution and maybe impose a one-party state. But as things remains in Namibia, it is largely a one- party dominance. The fear is well founded given the experiences in Zimbabwe, Angola and Mozambique but the changed international climate and the on-going euphoria for multi-party democracy in Africa will no doubt give SWAPO leaders some food for thought and a restrains on their desire for ultimate control of the Namibian body politic. The prevailing continental political climate do induce an indirect caution that leaders should work toward the preservation of a democratic Namibian state.

*————

~ 92.3% of the voters in ovamboland voted for SWAPO
~ 14.4% in Hereroland and 10% in Kaokoland voted for   SWAPO
~ 26% in Damaraland voted SWAPO while the UDF had 54.6%
~ 20% voted for SWAPO in Mariental and Bethanie(Namas) while the DTA had 57% and 56% respectively.

NOTES:

1. Abraham, K.(1980),"Representative Authority and Ethnic Elections" *Namibian Review,* july/August 1980(Windhoek, Namibia).
2. Dollie,N.(ed)(1988),*A Political Review of Namibia: Nationalism in Namibia*(Cape town,SA: logo Print)
3. Kiljunen,M-L.(1981),"The land and its Peoples"in Green, R.H.,Kiljunen, K. & Kiljunen, M-L,(ed),*Namibia: The Last Colony*(Essex,England:Longman).
4. Manning,P.(1989),*The UN Plan for Election in Namibia* (London:South Cain).
5. Moleah,A.T.(1983) *Namibia: The struggle for Liberation* (Wilmington,DE: Disa Press).
6. Ndegera,P.(1985),*Africa's Development Crisis*(Nairobi, Kenya: Heineman).
7.. Ojo,B.A.(1997)"The Military and the Democratization Process in Africa" A paper presented at the NorthEast Political Science Association Annual Meeting. Philadelphia, PA. (November 1997)
          (1992)"Nigeria and the French Perspectives on the South African Question" in Jacob,H. & Omar,M. (*1992)France and Nigeria: Issues in Comparative Studies* (Ibadan,Nigeria: CREDU/Documents in Social Sciences & Humanities).
          (1991)"SWAPO et l'independance de la Namibie: Une etude d'un mouvement de la liberation nationale(SWAPO and the Independence of Namibia: A study of a National liberation Movement),*Doctoral Dissertation*(Bordeaux,France:University of Bordeaux/CEAN).
          (1989)"Namibie vers l'independance"*Annee Africaine*(CEAN,Bordeaux/Edition Pedone,Paris).
          (1988) "La decolonisation de la namibie: Un etude de la politique interne(The decolonization of Namibia: A study of the internal political dynamics) *M.Phil Dissertation* (Bordeaux, France: University of Bordeaux/CEAN).
12]. Oyugi,W.O & Gitonga,A.(1987)*The Democratic Theory & Practice in Africa*(Nairobi,Kenya: Heineman).
13).Steckamp,W.(*1989)South Africa's Border Wars 1966-1989*(Gilbraltar: Ashanti publ.)
14]. SWAPO,(1989)"Election Manifesto: Toward an Independent & Democratic Namibia"(Windhoek,Namibia: SWAPO Policy Position)
15]. Totemeyer,G.(1989)"The Prospect for Democracy and Development In An Independent Namibia" *Research Paper,*#1(Namibia institute for Social & Economic Research).

Chapter 7

The Transition To Democracy In Nigeria: Engaging New Possibilities In A Changing World Order.

Austin Ogunsuyi

Introduction

Nigerians have gone to the polls and elected officials to represent them at the local government level.[1] They are scheduled to return to the polls again soon, to vote for representatives at the national level of government, if all goes well with General Sani Abacha's plans to hand over government to civilians. A legion of skeptics have joined the pool of optimists who are demonstrating an unusual level of resilience and faith in General Abacha's promise to hand over to civilians in October 1998, then he died suddenly in June 1998.. General Abacha stuck to a time table for the smooth transition, which would have lead to the swearing-in of a civilian president on October 1, 1998. But for a few glitches and delays, which occurred during the earlier rounds of the proposed handing over program and until his death everyone was resign to the idea that Abacha 's transition program remains the only but certain path to a Nigeria's civilian administration.

If transition from the military to civilians in Nigeria seem that sure it might be unnecessary to spend much time evaluating and speculating about an already predictable outcome. Not so for Nigeria. With the memories of June 12, 1993 still fresh in our minds we know better than jump to conclusions here.

Engaging New Possibilities

Just as in the final moments of the crippled attempt of the Babangida regime's handing over process, a lot of credit has been showered on the Abacha regime transition program, by both scholars and pundits. Many have argued that in a decade that has seen the demise of the nefarious apartheid regime in South Africa and the humiliation of Africa's most notorious dictator, Mobutu Sese Seko of former Zaire, it might after all make much sense to expect another `miracle' in the making, this time in Nigeria. Other optimists are hoping that Nigeria will follow the trend of recent success stories like Republic d' Benin, South Africa, Botswana and Ghana.

Given the foregoing, various levels of new possibilities could emanate, among them:

1) A smooth transition to a civilian government

2) popular acceptance of the new government

3) General Abacha becomes civilian President (this proposition is no longer viable since the general died on June the 8th, 1998.)

4) Chief M.K.O Abiola would head a transition team (He also died on July 6, 1998)

5) Another General steps in to replace Abacha (upon his death Abacha was replaced by Gen. Abdusallam Abubakar)

A Changing World Order

In "Democratic Experiments in Africa," Walle and Nicholas wonders whether the series of transitions to democracy in African in the 1990s could be considered a watershed.[2] They stated, "Political change certainly occurred. For the first time in the postcolonial era the trend toward the centralization of political power at the apex of the state was halted and partially reversed." They also noted that Africa's period of transition was marked not only by greater electoral competition and the ouster of incumbents but sometimes by fundamental changes in the rule of the political game. Larry Diamond and Marc in Civil Military Relation and

Democracy also remarked," The concluding years of the twentieth century have been marked by three historic developments that have transformed the political world; the spread of democracy, the collapse of Soviet communism, and the end of cold war."[3] In their opinion, the impact of the three momentous development led to the break down of the old conceptual division of the globe into first, second and third worlds. In their words, "With demise of the Soviet Union, not only one of the superpowers but the entire second world has disappeared. Many (though by no means all) countries that had been considered part of the Third World are now studied under the rubric of "new" or "emerging" democracies, category that also subsumes the postcommunist countries."[4]

In "Democratic Moment" Marc Plattner is more direct in his observation saying,"The dramatic events of August 1991 in Moscow should convince any remaining skeptics that the democratic revolutions of 1989 indeed marked a watershed in world history. The democratic tide swept through most of Latin America, reached such key Asian countries as the Philippines, Korea, Taiwan and Pakistan, and by decade's end was beginning to make ripples in sub-Saharan Africa and even Middle East."[5]

Focus of the Study

This chapter seeks to evaluate the transition program of the Abacha government. Some of the questions that should be answered will include 1) what are the prospects of smooth transition to civil rule? 2) what lessons can be learnt from preceding transition programs of Olusegun Obasanjo and Ibrahim Babangida? and 3) what are the likely extenuating circumstances that will could affect the outcome of the transition program. It would be informative to establish the social, cultural and political factors under which these transition programs were designed in order to determine the immediate and remote causes for their success or failure. As much of the projections will be based largely on the public actions and statements of the military rulers, efforts will be made to establish some basis for making some projections based on those public statements and

comments of other informed persons about their character and
predictability.[6]

A 50% Probability rate:

Coming out of the botched Babangida transition plan which had
hitherto received a wide acclaim, it must be prudent to refrain from
making absolute statements about military-civilian transition program in
Nigeria. Luckily, the smooth Obasanjo transition program leaves some
hope, no matter how little, of making a transition from military to civilian
administration. Although the Babangida regime failed to make a complete
transfer of power to a civilian regime, it non-the-less transferred power to
a civilian and took a bow.[7] That gesture was both symbolic as well as
substantive. To attribute the transition with 50% success because it led to
the exit of Babangida is appropriate and considerate. From the foregoing,
reducing the possibility index to real numbers will place Nigeria within
the range of a 50% chance of success at achieving transition from military
to civilian administration. That's not a passing grade.

Transition to Democracy:

In this chapter transition to democracy is discussed as the transfer of
power from the   military regime to a properly constituted civilian
administration. In "Democratic Experiments in Africa," Michael Bratton
and Nicolas van de Walle[8] explained:

> " A regime transition is a shift from one set of political procedures to
> another from an old pattern of rule to a new one. It is an interval of
> intense political uncertainty during which the shape of the new
> institutional dispensation is up for grabs by incumbent and opposition
> contenders."

They further stressed that transition may occur by means of a short,
sharp transformation, for example, when a coercive autocracy collapses

and give way to an elected democracy. Or a transition may unfold incremental, as when a personal dictatorship gradually relaxes controls on its political opponents and introduces a softer, more liberalized form of authoritarian rule. They also warn that the direction of transitions is multivalent, potentially unfolding toward harder more authoritarian regime types. This chapter will avoid the extensive debate over how much or less African societies or transition to civil rule can be considered as democratic and support Bratton and Walle in preferring the procedural definition of democracy because political regimes are best understood as sets of rules. As Ake notes: "It is the involvement in the process rather than the acceptability of the end decision, which satisfies the right to participate."[9]

The general objective of this study is to understand the reason why transition to civil rule is possible in some cases but not in others. A particular case in point would be to assess the successful transition by the Obasanjo regime to Alhaji Shehu Shagari administration, and the failure of the Babangida regime to carry out its planned transition to civil rule but failed. According to Donald Share:

> The support for democratization can be manifest in two ways:
> Authoritarian leaders may simply tolerate democratic political
> change, refraining from active stewardship over it; or they actively
> participate in the process of change, hoping thereby either to
> control and limit such change; or to forestall more distasteful change.[10]

The Olusegun Obasanjo, Ibrahim Babangida, and now General Sanni Abacha regimes all possess traits which could be disproved or verified by the foregoing assumptions. We shall now review some crucial aspects in the three regimes and their transition programs.

Olusegun Obasanjo Regime

Preamble:

Olusegun Obasanjo regime was the continuation of the Murtala Muhammed regime which came into office following a successful coup that ousted Major-General Yakubu Gowon. One of the reasons given for the deposition of Gowon was his decision to postpone the proposed return to civilian rule in 1976. Welch has argued that one of the factors favoring disengagement is a decisive event.[11] The July 1975 coup and leadership change was the decisive event in the Nigerian context. It stopped the drift in the direction of military rule for an indefinite period and makes a reassertion of commitment to disengagement as an immediate objective.[12]

Thus, the Murtala Muhammed regime turned its attention early to formulating a program for disengagement which was announced on October 1, 1975. The four year five stage program promised civilian rule by October , 1979.

Details of the time table[13] are as follows.

Stage 1:

> Appointment of a Constitutional Drafting Committee in October work on the preliminary draft.

Stage II

> Creation of new states and establishment of the newly created states by April 1976;
> completion first draft of the constitution by September 1976.

Stage III

> Election into a Constituent Assembly in October 1977.

Stage IV

Ratification of the Draft Constitution by the Constituent Assembly by October 1978 and lifting of the 1996 ban on political parties.

Stage V

States and Federal elections by 1979.
As part of the disengagement process, a number of other measures were taken by the Olusegun Obasanjo regime.

Politicians were dropped from membership of the federal and state executive committees, as from July 1975 and commissioners at federal and state level who may have future political ambition were asked to resign. By August 1978, military governors and military officers who were commissioners had been reassigned to military duties in an effort at "psychological disengagement" while a number of senior officers, including the Head of State, were to retire on the inception of a civilian administration. Also, efforts were intensified to complete the barracks to ensure that all military personnel are in barracks by 1979; while demobilization of some members of the armed forces was embarked upon. On the whole, the regime made every effort towards ensuring the completion of the transition program on schedule.

Ibrahim Babangida Regime

Preamble:

The Babangida administration came into existence following a "palace coup" which replaced Muhammed Buhari/Babatunde Idiagbon leadership in August, 1985. The major rationalization for the palace coup led by Major General Ibrahim Babangida was the alleged absence of a clear commitment by Buhari/Idiagbon to restore the economy and articulate a political program which would pave the way for a quick return to civil rule. On coming to power, the Babangida administration promised a new and viable political order which will be "strong enough to withstand the shock of political crisis while being flexible enough to adapt to desirable changes." To this end, a Political Bureau was inaugurated on January 13, 1986. The objectives included:

a) review the country's political history and identify the
basic problems which have led to past institutional   failure.
b) collect information from the public on these issues;
collate and evaluate these public contributions.

The Bureau submitted its report in May 18, 1987. The publication and announcement of a government white paper on the report was used as an opportunity to announce the government's transition to civil rule program. The political program for the country was formally announced to the nation in an address by the President on July 1, 1987. Among the things, the program contained a schedule or time table of activities which must be accomplished, or at least effectively institutionalized. beginning of the third quarter of 1987, before the disengagement by the armed forces in the forth quarter of 1992 which was later changed to 1993. The time table for transition to civil rule is presented below.

Time Table for Transition to Civil Rule 1987-1992[14]

Schedule I (Program for 1987)

3rd Quarter 1987

> Establishment of the Directorate of Social Mobilization
> Establishment of a National Electoral Commission
> Establishment of Constitution Drafting Committee

4th Quarter 1987

> Elections in the Local Governments on non-party basis

Schedule II (Program for 1988)

Ist Quarter 1988

> Establishment of National Population Commission
> Establishment of Code of Conduct Bureau
> Establishment of Code of Conduct Tribunal
> Inauguration of National revenue Mobilization Commission

2nd Quarter 1988

> Termination of Structural Adjustment Program (SAP)

3rd Quarter 1988

> Consolidation of gains of SAP

4th Quarter 1988

> Consolidation of gains of SAP.

Schedule III (Program for 1989)

Ist Quarter 1989

> Promulgation of a new Constitution
> Release of new fiscal arrangements

2nd Quarter 1989

> Lift of ban on party politics

3rd Quarter 1989

> Announcement of two recognized and registered political
> parties

4th Quarter 1989

> Election into Local Government on party basis

Schedule IV (Program for 1990)

Ist and 2nd Quarter 1990

> Election into State Legislatures and State Executives.

3rd Quarter 1990

> Convening of State Legislature

4th Quarter 1990

Swearing in of State Executives
Schedule V (Program for 1991)

1st Quarter 1991
Census

2nd Quarter 1991
Census

3rd Quarter 1991
Census

4th Quarter 1991
Local Government Elections

Schedule VI (Program for 1992)

1st and 2nd Quarters 1992
Elections in Federal Legislatures and convening of National
Assembly

3rd and 4th Quarters 1992

Presidential Election
Swearing-in-ceremony of new President and final
disengagement by Armed Forces.

Sani Abacha Transition Program

Preamble:

General Sani Abacha came into office riding the tide of one of the
worst turbulent moment in the nation's history. The presidential elections
staged by President Ibrahim Babangida failed to produce a president. A
series of court rulings by an Abuja High Court, supposedly incapacitated
the National Electoral Commission (NEC). The NEC stopped after it had
released results from fourteen states. The stalemate persisted even after
other high courts largely in southern states of the country denounced the

Abuja High court ruling and ordered that the rest of the results be released.

In the midst of these legal confusion, President Babangida annulled the election. His explanation was that there was need to save the judiciary from making a fool of itself.[15] He repealed the electoral decree under which the election was conducted. The annulment unleashed an unprecedented wave of crisis across the nation.

Pro-democracy advocates alleged complicity in the electoral process and openly called for the handing over of government to the front runner Alhaji M.K.O Abiola a southerner. The government held its ground on the annulment and refused to comply with the request of the pro-democracy groups. An unprecedented wave of crisis broke out in Lagos and many other cities in the South to force the Babangida regime to install Alhaji Abiola as president. Instead, President Babangida hastily swore-in and handed over the reins of affairs to an interim government under the leadership of Chief Ernest Shonekan. Rather than assuage the wrath of warring pro-democracy groups, the situation took a turn for the worse. The new government did not enjoy the confidence of the populace. As Chief Shonekan interim government was crippled by a series of judicial decisions he resigned and General Abacha a leading member of the interim took over.[16]

Speaking at a Chief of Army Staff conference in December 1993, General Sani Abacha said,

> No military worth its salt can fold its arms while the country it has sworn to defend is fast plunging into abyss of disintegration. The military has the onerous responsibility to ensure the return of normalcy and create a conducive atmosphere for the emergence of a sustainable democratic polity.[17]

General Abacha announced a three-year transition program on October 1, 1995.

Details are as follows:

1995 Last Quarter - October-December

Approval of Draft Constitution
Lifting all restrictions on Political Activities
Establishment of National Electoral Commission of Nigeria
(NECON)
Creation of:
      Transitional Implementation Committee
      National Reconciliation Commission
      Federal Character Commission
Appointment of Panel for Creation of State; Local
Government; Boundary Adjustment

1996 First Quarter January - March

Election and inauguration of Local Government Councils on
Party Basis.

1996 Second Quarter April - June

Creation of States and Local Governments
Commences process on Political Party Registration

1996 Third Quarter July - September

Registration of Political Parties
Delineation of Constituencies
Production of authentic Voters Register

1996 Fourth Quarter October - December

Election of Local Government Councils at Party Level

1997 First Quarter January - March

Inauguration of Party elected Local Government Councils
Consolidation of new Political Party structures
Tribunal sitting and conduct of any local Government Bye
Elections

1997 Second Quarter April - June

Party-State Primaries to select Candidates for State
Assembly and Governorship Elections.
Screening and approval of Candidates by the National
Electoral Commission of Nigeria.

1997 Third Quarter July - September

State Assembly Elections.

1997 Fourth Quarter October - December

Election of State Governors
Sitting of State Elections Tribunals and conduct of Bye
Election.

1998 First Quarter January - March

Inauguration of State Assembly and Governors
Party Primaries to select Candidates for National Assembly
Elections
National Assembly Election Campaigns

1998 Second Quarter April - June

National Assembly Elections
Primaries to select Candidates for Presidential Elections
Commencement of Nationwide Campaigns for the Presidential
Elections.

1998 Third Quarter July - September

Presidential Elections

1st October 1998

Swearing-in of new President and final disengagement.

Similarities In The Three Transition Programs.

In all three transition programs, obvious aspects of similarities stand out. Among these similarities are:

    1) Undergirding philosophy of the program.
    2) ideological commitment
    3) Constitution Ratification
    4) creation of States

1) Undergirding Philosophy of the Transition Program:

The same philosophy of military disengagement informs both transition programs. The major difference; one succeeded and the other did not. In his address to the nation on October I, 1975, the then Head of State Murtala Muhammed announced:

"The present military leadership does not intend to stay in office a day longer than necessary."[18]

Commenting on the virtues of military professionalism, Obasanjo notes:

"For those of us who count on institutional integrity and credibility for the military and defense for the unity and integrity of Nigeria our words on behalf of that institution must be matched by our actions....."[19]

Similarly, Babangida explained:

We inherited a Western liberal model of civil-military relations from the British. This model of civil-military relations exhorted civilian supremacy. It provided for an apolitical professional military whose place was in the barracks, protecting and defending the integrity of the nation and its people.[20]

In Nigeria, the process of so called disengagement entailed a planned period of transition from military to civilian rule. President Babangida explained:

On the whole, the emphasis in this type of approach to demilitarization is on constitutional and methodological procedure of military disengagement. It involves drawing up an elaborate time-table for a phased return to civilian rule...., and finally the holding of national elections to determine the civilian successors to the military.[21]

Speaking in a similar vein, President Abacha noted:

The present transition program will be a test and it should be a discovery that a new and cherished spirit has emerged among our leaders of tomorrow. As we embark on this crucial stage our transition, this Administration is fully committed to the task of its implementation.[22]

This common characteristic manifest during the Olusegun Obasanjo administration, was premised on a transitional disengagement process and phased over four years (1975-1979), seem to be repeated in the disengagement program of Babangida regime, which was phased over seven years (1986-1993); it also comes close to that proposed by the Sani Abacha regime which was phased over three years (1995-1995).

2) Ideological Commitment:

In terms of ideology, of government, Obasanjo and Babangida and Abacha share similar view that portrays them as representing the core values of a conservative army. In terms of economic arrangement, Socialism was never considered an option throughout the phases of the transition programs, leaving the way for the capitalist ideology and government, Obasanjo, then Head of State, pointed out:

Because socialism is a younger doctrine and a reaction to capitalism, it has proved to be more attractive to all who seek change and has been described as "progressives" while the word "conservative" has been associated with capitalism. I do not intend to go into the semantics of the terms "conservative" and "progressive," but I would like to say categorically that rather than clarify, they tend to confuse issues.[23]

He further stated:

I am convinced beyond all doubts that the decision to choose between capitalism and socialism and energy expanded in making this choice becomes diversionary and wasted. The alternative to this mirage is to achieve, through efficient management our capacity for qualitative and quantitative improvements.[24]

General Sani Abacha equally alluded to his commitment to the status quo by saying:

Within the period of transition therefore, Government will maintain a policy of consolidation of the economic reforms which have had such a remarkable success. These include the broadening and strengthening of our revenue base, control of expenditure of reduced fiscal deficit; reduction of the rate of inflation; guided deregulation of the foreign exchange market; and protection of the balance of payments to support economic activities.[25]

Similarly, while commenting on the findings and recommendations of the Political Bureau, President Babangida asserted inter alia, that:

We did not accept the socialist ideology that informed their action. We did so believing that the principles enshrined in the 1979 constitution contained ideas that could form a philosophy for any progressive government. We believe that what went wrong in the past was not the lack of ideas but the absence of guiding principles and practices on which genuine political parties could operate.[26]

It is therefore obvious from the above statements by Obasanjo,

Babangida and Abacha that they implicitly endorse the present arrangement in Nigeria. This, by implication means that socialism will not have much hope on their agenda. It also by default implies that military disengagement programs possess an ideological character, or a commitment to the maintenance of the inherited, neocolonial political economy and values.

3) Constitution Ratification:

Like the one preceding it, under the present transition program, a Constitution Drafting Committee (CDC) was set up and has produced a constitution which is similar in many respects to the 1979 constitution. As in 1978, a Constituent Assembly (CA) was constituted to produce the final draft of the constitution. Also, the two transition programs share certain similarities in terms of the method of constituting members of the Constitution Drafting Committee and Constituent Assembly as well as the composition of the two bodies. For example, during preparation for the second republic in Nigeria, the Constitution Drafting Committee was hand-picked by the military authorities mainly from the elite class. The Constituent Assembly (CA) which was partly elected and partly nominated had no place for the masses-whether as individuals or on representational basis.

The Babangida transition program turns out to a parody of the preceding one. The Constitution Drafting Committee was hand picked by the military authorities from the intelligentsia - business - commercial class. The Constituent Assembly was partly nominated by government (117 members) and partly elected (450 members). It is important to point out that although the elected members are in the majority, they do not really represent the Nigerian electorate. A former president of the Nigerian Bar Association said, "the electoral college itself is faulty because it was rushed. The government predetermined the assembly by sending nominees who could represent their interest."

Abacha transition program equally convened a broad-based national conference to discourse and make recommendations to rectify the constitution. As was the case in the Babangida regime Abacha led Provisional Ruling Council reserved the sole authority to rectify the recommendations of the National Constitutional Conference. One remarkable difference in the new constitution is the provision for a president, vice-president, a prime minister and a deputy prime minister. All these offices in addition to the senate presidency and Speaker of the house of representatives will rotate among the six zones in the country.[27]

State Creation:

Both Olusegun Obasanjo and Ibrahim Babangida regimes made state creation an important aspect of their transition to civil rule programs. Thus on February 3, 1976, the then Head of State Murtala Muhammed announced in a dawn broadcast, the creation of seven new states. The decision to create new States followed the government's consideration of the report of a panel by Mr. Justice Irikefe, which travelled the country hearing evidence, and brought the number of States in the country to nineteen.

Similarly, under the Babangida regime, additional eleven States excluding Abuja had been created in Nigeria bringing the number to thirty States.

General Abacha also gave State Creation a top priority. As the Constitutional Conference could not resolve the issue of creation of states and local government, Abacha led Provisional Ruling Council took the responsibility upon itself. A committee assigned for the task examined various requests and at the end the Abacha regime announced the creation of six more states.

Differences in the Transition Programs among the Three Regimes.

Aside from the similarities already mentioned, certain basic differences exist in the transition programs of Obasanjo, Babangida and Abacha regimes. The basic differences are as follows:

1) Duration and emphasis of the transition program
2) The nature of political participation
3) Economic and Political questions
4) Party Politics
5) Census

1) Phasing and the Transition program.

The most important distinguishing feature between the Abacha, Babangida Obasanjo transition programs is the time frame for return to civilian rule. Abacha proposes three years, while Babangida needed seven years and Obasanjo succeeded in five years. Somehow Abacha is laying emphasis on the a supervised return to civil rule which was the hallmark of the failed Babangida program. In his 1996 budget speech, President Babangida critique certain aspects of the first disengagement prog ram of Olusegun Obasanjo military regime, especially in terms of its modus operandi and modus vivendi, and the basic assumptions that informed it.

He had noted that leaving room for mistakes and improper supervision of disengagement led to the failure of the succeeding civilian regime. It was also on that basis that President Babangida proffered a different approach to the politics of disengagement which provided that the military should "monitor and supervise" those who were to succeed them as "players in the game of politics."

Almost in an identical manner the Abacha regime noted that it step-in to rescue the nation from lack of effective leadership and chaos.

From the foregoing discussion, the main points in the intention and mechanics of disengagement was thus confirmed. We saw how Obasanjo raised a critical question about the basic assumptions underlying the second disengagement program, while asserting that the assumptions were a threat to the "credibility and integrity of the military institution."[28]

In all, whatever risk was involved in the "gradual detail by detail" transition program of Babangida, it was guided by the desire to avoid the mistakes of the past. Somehow, General Abacha seem to come closer to the view point raised by Obasanjo, which questioned the integrity of a military's prolonged disengagement program. But he also affirmed The armed forces have the onerous responsibility to ensure the return of normalcy and create a conducive atmosphere for the emergence of a sustainable democratic polity.[29]

2) The question of political participation:

The attitude of the various regimes to the old politicians also differs. As we noted earlier in this paper, all three regime claim that their transition programs were informed by past experiences and the desire to provide a lasting solution to political instability and provide a political climate that would disengage the military "permanently" from Nigerian politics.The Babangida administration viewed the problems of democracy in Nigeria as the handiwork of politicians and not so much the lack of a sound constitutional framework. He sought therefore to seek ways of keeping politicians in check by engaging a supervisory role over their affairs during the transition process. According to the President Babangida, and much to the relief of millions of Nigerians:

> We shall not entrust the destiny of our great nation to a group of politicians who will crush her national interest under the jackboot of ignorance and selfishness.[30]

Although the ban was lifted after the Governorship election in December 1991, it remained an important difference between Obasanjo and Babangida's transition program. Under Olusegun Obasanjo administration, such a ban did not exist. During the duration of the ban, only the so-called "New Breed Politicians" participated in the local government, state legislature and gubernatorial elections.
Abacha in dealing with the issue of politicians in office, seem to have borrowed a leaf from both previous transition plan. Elected officers at the local government levels will experience some level of supervision from the military under Abacha regime, but it will be for a shorter period of time as during the Babangida administration.

3) Economies and Politics

The Babangida transition program looked to reviving the nation's economy through an adherence to the Structural Adjustment Program (SAP).
But the Abacha regime is emphasizing more fiscal discipline and the deregulation of the foreign exchange market. At the same time in a practice reminiscent of the Babangida transition program Abacha has strive to make mass participation and mobilization the corner stone of his transition program. He courted and incorporated an unprecedented number of intellectuals, educators and former politicians in the program.
Obasanjo relied on a representative constitution drafting committee and later on Constituent Assembly and engaged on Programs such as Universal Primary Education, Operation Feed the Nation and Low Profile' to court popular support and legitimacy for his program; Babangida employed the tactics of mass participation and mass mobilization as a

modality of gaining (courting) support and legitimacy for his program. Thus while Obasanjo relied solely on bureaucratic government institution run by civil servants to carry out his programs, Babangida started his program by first mobilizing the entire populace for a national debate on the political future of the country. Since then he has sought to energize the entire populace into his political program.

He established bodies like - Directorate of Food, Roads and Rural Infrastructure (DFRRI), National Directorate of Employment (NDE) and Mass Mobilization for Social Justice and Economic Recovery (MAMSER) must be seen not as one of those exercises in institution proliferation but as charged with the responsibility of ensuring that the mass of the people identify with the goals and aspirations of the government. In similar practice the Abacha administration established the National Electoral Commission of Nigeria, NECON, the Political Transition Implementation Committee, the Committee on creation of States and local governments and boundary adjustments, the Federal Character Commission, the National Reconciliation Committee and the Committee on Devolution of Powers between the Federal State and local governments.

An obvious corner stone to Abacha strategy for gaining popular support was to attract prominent civilians to participate in one form or another. The National Constitutional Conference attracted such personalities as Dr. Alex Ekwueme, vice president in second republic; Chukwuemeka Odumegwu-Ojukwu who led the Biafran secession; Umaru Dikko, Shagari's powerful minister of transport, Major Shehu Musa Yar Adua, Chief of Staff Supreme Headquarters in the Obasanjo administration as well as traditional rulers, leading politicians, retired senior military officers, as well as technocrats.[31]

4) Party Politics

Although all transition programs profess their commitment to party politics, their approaches were fairly different. Babangida cut down the number of parties to two but Abacha has approved eighteen political parties.

Babangida's reasons for reducing the number of political parties to two were elaborated in the political bureau report:

a) elimination of sectionalism by making parties as integrative political organs that will encourage the forging of national consensus;

b) facilitating choice by the electorate through limiting the choice of party candidates to two instead of the previous numerous candidates that confused the electoral scene; and

c) encouraging the parties to sharpen their respective program focuses in order to make the choice clear for the electorate.

This time around of the twenty-three political associations which collected application eighteen of them returned the forms to the commission; and five were officially registered. Speculations that Abacha could be touting running for office of president remain very high among the newly formed political parties. Nearly all of them are reportedly reserving their number one spot for Abacha when he would supposedly declare his candidacy.[32] Despite Abacha's denial of any intention to run for president the rumors have remain very popular.

All three regimes under consideration have fervently argued against repeating the mistakes of the past when political parties were mostly organized from the top downwards, in which case, leaders emerged first and then usually went around the country to generate the followers or agents at the local levels. Past political parties were also often described as loose coalitions of narrow interest and solidarity groups which were put together for purely selfish reasons. The leaders of the parties were also blamed for acting as owners of the political parties.

These proclivities on the part of the political party leaders, according to the military rulers, affected the degree of democracy within the parties, and the manner in which those political parties behaved in their operation as institutions of government.

As soon as the ban on party politics was lifted, the Babangida military government assumed full ownership of the two political parties. Every Nigerian 18 years and older, except those citizens who were banned or disqualified from political activity, is free to register and contest election. Thus, it was supposed, for the first time since independence, the Nigerian citizen was to some extent been truly elevated to equal partners in determining the political destiny of his/her country.

Abacha like Babangida took the liberty of cutting down the number of applicants for party registration.

Census

Unlike the Obasanjo transition program, the Babangida regime made the conduct of a national census an important component of its transition program. The census was conducted in November 1991, and the result has been released to the public.

Neither Obasanjo nor Abacha regimes considered the census as a matter of immediate attention.

Concluding Remarks

In this chapter, we have compared and contrasted the transition programs of Olusegun Obasanjo, Ibrahim Babangida and Sani Abacha(in Nigeria) with the sole objective of revealing any remarkable characteristics for their proper evaluation and review. Most importantly, as the Abacha regime proposal is still in the future it could afford the rare privilege of a glimpse at the possible outcome. Without a doubt, and as was rightly noted by Professor Oyeleye Oyediran:

> "The difference between the first and the second have been the out-
> come of the objective conditions in which they were conceived, and
> the dramatis personae involved in the design and implementation of
> both programs."[33]

The ugly experiences of the past administration somehow influenced and motivated the new measures taken in subsequent attempts at democracy. Structurally, it has become more difficult to judge a transition program on its face value after the collapse of the widely acclaimed Babangida transition program. It is therefore impossible to discern the outcome of a transition program by looking merely at the structure of the program itself. But, we shall none-the-less, attempt some of the pertinent questions posed earlier, viz:

1) what are the prospects of smooth transition to civil rule?

2) what lessons can be learnt from preceding transition programs of Olusegun Obasanjo and Ibrahim Babangida? and

3) what are the likely extenuating circumstances that could affect the outcome of the transition program.

1)What are the prospects of smooth transition to civil rule?

Given the unpredictable nature of politics in Nigeria, it would be
nearly impossible to determine the outcome of a transition program by
merely looking at the structure of the program or the promises of the
military leaders. In terms of design and philosophical foundation the
Babangida transition program seemed superior to any other. But the
Obasanjo transition program that was not as detailed nor informed by the
same technical deft as the Babangida transition program is the only one
that has succeeded so far. That means the Abacha regime transition
program, although seemly rushed and less detailed as the Babangida
transition program, could succeed.

A more important factor that could work to the advantage to the
Abacha regime transition program is the changing world order. As
discussed earlier on page 130, the wave of democracy blowing across a
post-cold war world has witnessed an unprecedented transformation of
many autocratic governments into democracy. It would be mindful to warn
against assuming with certainty the success of the transition program
because of the changing world order. It would be worthy to recall that the
Babangida transition program crumbled at the peak of the new wave of
transition to democracy in 1993.

2)What lessons can be learnt from the Babangida transition   program?

The foremost lesson to be learnt from the Babangida transition
program is "surprise" and "irresolute" nature of politics in Nigeria. From
what we learn from major players in the Babangida transition program
some entity quite unpredictable emanated at the seventh hour to lay claim
to the helm of power. In an interview with Tell, a Nigerian based
magazine Professor Omo Omoruyi who headed the Center for Democratic
Studies under the Babangida regime, blamed a highly politicized military
that have reduced civilian politicians to purchasable items.
Prof Omo Omoruyi said the Babangida transition program was not
designed to produce an interim government but to produce an elected
president.[34] He said a cadre of military generals mainly from Northern
Nigeria intercepted that program when it was clear that a southerner,
M.K.O Abiola was going to win. In his comments on the June 12
annulment, Nobel Peace Laureate Wole Soyinka said, the "robust
detonation" of the myth of the North-South dichotomy took place finally

on June 12, 1993.[35]

3) What are the extenuating circumstances that could affect the outcome of the transition program.

From the foregoing, the most likely circumstance that could impede the transition to democracy in 1998, is when a southerner or someone outside the core of Abacha's choice candidates, wins or is winning the presidential elections. Here, a few words about the personality of Abacha would be informative. According to the New York Times, the 52-year old leader has been near the forefront of his country's military dominated politics for two decades, making and breaking governments.[36] In the words of one diplomat, Abacha does not seem to have the love of power that Babangida had, all one can think of is that he wants an insurance policy that will let him hang on to his ill gotten wealth.

A resurgence of the pro-democracy forces that erupted after the annulment of June 12, might also be pandered as an excuse for termination of the transition program. As always in Nigeria, you cannot rule out the insurrection of a brand new cadre of ambitious military junta waiting eagerly to continue the loot where others have left off. This third possibility is most remote.

Lessons from Abacha's most provocative decisions.

Any student of politics looking at the decisions made by Abacha so far would find many inconsistencies that would make a framework for an easy prediction of his future actions or reactions. Nonetheless, looking at some of his decisions will reveal some indications of his most cherished commitments as a military ruler. From all indication Abacha has made no secret of his intention to be perceived as a military strongman. In the opinion of many analysts, the Abacha regime has gone further than any previous regimes in abrogating civil rights, repressing civil society by giving a virtual *carte blanc* to security forces. In the words of Wole Soyinka, "In Nigeria we have suffered day by day under the Abacha regime from kidnapping, hostage takings, state terrorism, the liquidation of media houses in a single blow, the regime's monopoly of the electronic media, and the desecration of the entire judicial structure."[37] Soyinka has since joined the growing number of Nigerian intellectuals who now reside overseas fearing reprisal from the Abacha regime.

In line with living up to its strongman image, Abacha's regime, despite worldwide appeals went on with the execution of environmentalist Ken Saro Wiwa and nine others who had protested against the activities of Shell Petroleum in Ogoni. Abacha did not only betray his desire to he perceived as a military strongman but that action equally confirmed his willingness to resist any attempt to interrupt the steady flow of income, from oil, that would guarantee his patronage system. On the international srage, Abacha has further displayed his desire to hold on to power at all cost including manipulating all forces at his disposal. Nigeria's recent involvement in Liberian crisis and Sierra Leone must be seen as deliberate strategies to assuage worldwide condemnation of Abacha's draconia domestic policies. In further pursuance of its strategy for improved image at the international level, the Abacha regime more than any other, has engaged in the most expensive propaganda crusade overseas, particularlly in the United States and Europe.

Most prominent among these efforts was the public relations battle which Abacha government officials have been waging over the naming of a New York City street in honor of the slain wife of political prisoner, M.K.O Abiola. From the foregoing it would appear that Abacha's desire to be perceived locally as a military strongman, and internationally as a progressive, who is willing to commit force for the course of democracy and peace, will ultimately compel him to carry through his plans for transition to civil-rule. What will come after that, could be anybody's guess. The next logical question to ask would be, how prepared are the pro-democracy forces to seize any opportunity, no matter how small, and establish an authentic civilian led government?. Unfortunately, the prospects of Nigeria's politicians uniting to forge a common front against the domination of the military seem quite remote.

Notes

1.Nigeria Today, "Local Government Elections-Cornerstone to Transition

Program," April-June 1997 vol.1 no. 1.

2.Michael Bratton and Nicolas van de Walle, *Democratic Experiment in Africa: Regime Transitions in Comparative Perspective*, (New York: Cambridge University, 1997), p. 7.

3.Larry Diamond and Marc Plattner (ed), Civil-Military Relation and Democracy,(Baltimore: The John Hopkins University Press 1996), P. ix.

4.Ibid.

5.Marc Plattner, "The Democratic Moment," *The Global Resurgence of Democracy*,(ed) Larry Diamond and Marc Plattner,(Baltimore: The John Hopkins University Press, 1996), p.3.

6.This model at best in its primitive form seeks to establish basis for predicting behavior using such factors as individual's concern for public perception, public image and integrity. The military and its officials must score high on the scale of such an evaluation because they profess to uphold the highest sense of duty and patriotism in any nation.

7.Babangida's exit is seen here as a partial victory for pro-democracy movement as it marked the first time in Nigeria's history, that a military strongman had succumb to public opinion and resorted to rather unusual damage control techniques which of necessity, brought his reign to an inglorious end.

8.Michael Bratton and Nicolas van de Walle, Democratic Experiments in Africa,(New York: Cambridge University Press, 1997), pg.10.

9. Ibid.

10.Donald Share, "Transition To Democracy and Transition Through Transition, *Comparative Political Studies*, vol. 19, No. 4. p. 29.

11. Claude E. Welch, *No Farewell To Arms*, Boulder Colorado: Westview Press, 1987), p. 20.

12. Banjo A.O. *The Potential for Military Disengagement from Politics: A Nigeria Case Study*, 1966-1979 (Lagos: NIIA, 1980); p29

13. Source: National Electoral Commission, Lagos. *It's equally important to note that there were changes to the time table. For instance, the swearing-in date for the new President which was originally scheduled for December 1992 was changed to January 1993.*

14. Source: Nigerian Government Documents, printed in Lagos.

15.*"Towards A New Nation: Abacha's Democratization Process,"* Government Document (Lagos, Nigeria: Academy Press Plc.)

16. Ibid., p. 11.

17. *Towards A New Nation: Abacha's Democratization Process*, (Lagos, Nigeria: Academy Press Pls), p. 10.

18. Oyeleye Oyediran (ed) *Survey of Nigeria Affairs 1975* (Lagos, Nigeria: International Affairs and Oxford University Press, 1978), p.31.

19. *Address by General Olusegun Obasanjo at the launching of the book "Diplomatic Soldering" by Major General Joe Garba on 26th November, 1987.*

20. *President Ibrahim Babangida's Budget Speech for 1986, in Lagos Nigeria.*

21.Ibid.

22. *Broadcast to the Nation by General Sani Abacha, 1st October, 1995, p. 19*
23."Discipline, Equality and Humanity," Speech by His Excellency, Lt. General Olusegun Obasanjo, Head of the Armed Forces at the formal opening of the Command and Staff College, Jaji on Monday, 12th September, 1977, p. 7.
24. Ibid.
25. *Broadcast to the Nation by General Sani Abacha, October 1st, 1995, p. 5.*
26. Ibid.
27. Towards a New Nation: Abacha's Democratization Process, (Lagos: Academy Press Plc), p.17.
28. Ibid
29. Towards a New Nation: Abacha's Democratization process, (Lagos: Academy Press Plc) p. 11.
30. *President Babangida's address to Senior Armed Forces Officers at Abuja on 17th October, 1987, p. 16*
31. Towards A New Nation: Abacha's Democratization Process, (Lagos: Academy Press Plc), p.16.
32. West Africa News, "Abacha Eyes Presidency," p.7.
33. Oyeleye Oyediran, *"The Gospel of the Second Change: A Comparison of Obasanjo and Babangida Military Disengagement in Nigeria."* Quarterly Journal of Administration, vol. 23, Nos 1 & 2, October, 1988 and January 1989.
34. Tell,"The Secret Pact," September 29, 1997

35. International Forum for Democratic Studies; Nigeria's Political Crisis: Which Way Forward? (National Endowment for Democracy D.C. February, 1995)
36. New York Times, "The leader is elusive" by Howard French, October 20, 1995 A.p.5 c.1.
37. International Forum For Democratic Studies: Nigeria's Political Crisis: Which Way Forward? (National Endowment for Democracy, DC 1995)

Bibliography
Address by General Olusegun Obasanjo at the launching of the book
        "Diplomatic Soldering" by Major General Joe Garba on
26th November, 1987.
Banjo A.O. *The Potential for Military Disengagement from Politics: A Nigeria Case Study,* 1966-1979 (Lagos: NIIA,   1980);
Broadcast to the Nation by General Sani Abacha, October 1st, 1995.
Claude E. Welch, *No Farewell To Arms,* Boulder Colorado: Westview Press, 1987).
Olusegun Obasanjo,"Discipline, Equality and Humanity," Speech by General Olusegun Obasanjo, Head of the Armed forces in Donald Share,
"Transition To Democracy and Transition Through Transition," *Comparative Political Studies,* vol. 19.
International Forum For Democratic Studies: Nigeria's Political Crisis: Which Way

Forward? Conference Report, (National Edowment for Democracy, 1995).

Larry Diamond and Marc Plattner (ed), *Civil-Military Relation and Democracy,* (Baltimore: The John Hopkins University Press 1996).

Marc Plattner, "The Democratic Moment," *The Global Resurgence of Democracy,* Larry Diamond and Marc Plattner(ed) (Baltimore: The John Hopkins University Press, 1996)

Michael Bratton and Nicolas van de Walle, *Democratic Experiments in Africa,* (New York: Cambridge University Press, 1997).

Oyeleye Oyediran, *"The Gospel of the Second Change: A Comparison of Obasanjo and Babangida Military Disengagement in Nigeria."* Quarterly Journal of Administration, vol. 23, Nos 1 & 2, October, 1988 and January 1989.

Nigeria Today, "Local Government Elections-Cornerstone to Transition Program," April-June 1997 vol.1 no. 1.

New York Times, "The leader is elusive" by Howard French, October 20, 1995.

.President Ibrahim Babangida's Budget Speech for 1986, in Lagos Nigeria.

President Babangida's address to Senior Armed Forces Officers at Abuja on 17th October, 1987.

Nigerian Government Documents, printed in Lagos.

Tell,"The Secret Pact: Towards A New Nation: Abacha's Democratization Process," September 29, 1997

Government Document (Lagos, Nigeria: Academy Press Plc.)

West Africa News, "Abacha Eyes Presidency."

Chapter 8

South Africa And Post Apartheid Democracy

Bamidele A. Ojo

The peace accord ,the election and the inauguration of Nelson Mandela as President plus the transition to post-apartheid South Africa was a product of extensive negotiations and socio- political and economic pressures both from within and outside Pretoria. But given the euphoria that surrounded the transition, we seek to examine the political reality amidst the high expectations in a post apartheid South Africa while examining the role of the state in post apartheid and democratic South Africa. The expectations that followed the transition were reminiscent of the earlier days of independence in many African states.

And the experience have since shown that , these types of expectations as high and intense and becomes unachievable within an expected period of time, which in turn could undermine nation-building and precipitate the beginning of the collapse of of sustainable democracy in South Africa. African independence remains a historical accomplishment of epochal dimension(Young, 1994) however, the colonial state was embedded in its post independence successor as a corrosive personality. The new South African state is no exception and it is a product of its predecessor- the apartheid state.

The apartheid state was not democratic. It was repressive and exploited its majority. It was racially segregated and characterized by legally supported inequality, with a white minority which dominated its black and African majority in all aspect of life. The accumulation of economic surplus which gave its whites minority population a standard of living comparable to those of the West, while Africans live in abject poverty.

The lucrative economic situation makes South Africa the Mecca of profit for multinational corporations and was anchored into place by the migrant labor system. The apartheid state was neither fair or just or respectful of the rights of its majority. The post-apartheid state cannot therefore be totally divorced from its predecessor because, the factors that makes states are embedded in the nature of the State itself, especially in the manner which it evolves and in the interests it represent(Shipo Shezi,1995). South Africa as a State has never enjoyed any legitimacy to exercise political authority. Its ideological framework have always raised questions challenging its legitimate authority over its people. It is difficult to perceive the successor state not inheriting many of these traits and which if care is not taken may suffer the same predicament- that of collapse, in terms of authority , law and order especially if one take cognizance of the fact that its legitimacy is still being challenged in many sections of the political landscape.

The white community which have used the state to entrench its supremacy and prosperity while at the same time hoping and holding steadfastly to their belief that the black majority which fought to dismantle the apartheid state because it violated their basic human rights might want to use it to redistribute the resources in the society for the benefits of all and to affirm the will of all. There is the need to build a new legitimacy in cooperation with every segments of the Society. The decline of the apartheid state began its gradual process of decline in the 1970s (Ohlson & Stedman,1994) This process gather momentum during the 1980s when it became clear that the state was unable to maintain law and order.

With the economy plummeting because of the flight of capital, domestic economic pressure, international isolation, economic and diplomatic sanctions and arms embargo, foreign debts and loss of international credit worthiness, the decline of the apartheid State was further hastened by the changing international system and the wars in Angola and Namibia(Sipho Shezi,1995:192). This situation was aggravated by the intensified mass struggle, boycotts and increased level of domestic political mobilization. Failure of last ditch political efforts to sustain the decaying state through establishment of black local authorities, mass detention and political trials and the failure of the homeland system, further damaged and undermine the basis of apartheid state.

But 1990 marked the turning point in South Africa history, with the release of Nelson Mandela ,the unbanning of the African National Congress[ANC] and the repealing of laws that have been the basis of the apartheid state. All these and the Multiparty talks (Congress for Democratic South Africa[CODESA]) were aimed at democratizing the South African State.

These development was followed by the suspension of armed struggle by both ANC and the Pan-African Congress(PAC) ,the eventual election of April 1994, and the formation of the transitional executive council. The election of April 26-29 1994 gave the majority its first taste of freedom and marked the end of the apartheid state.

But the end of the apartheid state and the holding of election do not automatically translate into the emergence of a democratic State. The elections were symbolic as well as Nelson Mandela becoming President but the new state carries within it the legacy of its predecessor. The legacy of political violence, the culture of confrontation, the defiance of authority, political intolerance   and deep seated racial animosity are all characteristics of South African political culture.

The question is how the new South African state will respond to its inherited legacies which was undermined its predecessor.For example, it will be difficult to build the trust between people and the police. The legitimacy of the legal system and the agents of the State is in question even though they might now be headed by black South Africans. The government headed by the ANC need to also adapt government institutions and to respond to the need of Africans(and especially its followers) , who anxiously await a dramatic change in their socio-economic status in the new society, at the same time protecting the interest of minorities.

The New State

Nelson Mandela as President of post-apartheid South Africa, is not only symbolic but capable of sustaining democratic change. He confers legitimacy on the new State and enhance the credibility of the government and its capacity to meet the needs of its citizens. The grey- haired patriarch is a much needed boost for creating a sense of national pride among the blacks and some member of the white community.

His achievements transcend the immediate international recognition of the new state. He not only consolidated his administration by filling his post with distinction in an attempt to advance national reconciliation but these positions were created with a sense of uniting the people of South Africa. He   opened up dialogue with the Afrikaner Resistance Movement(AWB) in an attempt to resolve crisis of legitimacy that could have fragmented the South African society.

For example, it is no mean achievement to bring the ANC, de Klerk's National Party and Mongisuthu Buthelezi's Inkatha Freedom Party into the government in the interest of stability and national unity. He refused to be drawn into party politics while obtaining wide ranging support for the ANC's election platform- the Reconstruction and Development Program to combat poverty and compensate the victim of apartheid. His leadership have minimized the prophesized political violence that was expected to lead South Africa into a state of anarchy. Violence continue in this new South Africa but have only diminished in intensity. For example, nearly 1400 people were killed in the 100 days leading to Mandela's inauguration on May 10 and the record for the 100 days of his Presidency shows a fewer than 500 people killed(Patrick Laurence,1994). The reduction in violence immediately following Mandela's inauguration is perhaps to provide the new government" an honeymoon" and as indicated below, there have since been a resurgence of violence in the new South Africa.

Mandela's administration successfully integrated the five regular army of the old South African Defense force and the defense force of the four defunct independent homelands, which were established under apartheid and the military units of the ANC and the PAC. This new South African National Defense force could effectively serve as a crucible where a new inclusive sense of nationhood could be built. But these achievements were offset by the legacies of the apartheid state such as cases involving the killing of policemen which is a carryover from de Klerk's administration . For example more than 180 policemen were murdered in 1994(Patrick Laurence, 1994). There have also been an increased trade union militancy and labor disputes became rampant to the extent that it was feared that the resulting industrial instability could lead to flight of investment.

Violence: A Legacy Of Apartheid.

There is no doubt about the fact that the violent conflict in the African communities endangers the delicate transition in South Africa. These violence are themselves a product of the apartheid state. Central to the apartheid regime was the indiscriminate use of violence against the black majority. This is further manifested in the division engineered in the African communities by the racist regime.The policy of " divise et reigne" worked so well that sections of the African community were absorbed into the apartheid regime's machines. They became effectively integrated in the racist state as a tool in the hand of the Afrikaners, in the effort to maintain their hegemony. Prominent among these groups were the Zulus and the Inkatha freedom movement led by Buthelezi. But the other groups including those represented by the ANC and other organizations have come to distrust the "collaborators".

The intense degree of distrust among South African is partly responsible for the present day violence that threatens the very existence of the post apartheid state. Another source of violence is the economic inequalities that continue to exist among blacks and whites. As usual and like in many other African state before them, many black South Africans have expected an immediate change in their socio-economic condition with the new state. But instead what they have witnessed is the increase in unemployment and stagnation in the economy. The continue poverty in the neighborhood became unacceptable and these have led to increase in crime, especially against affluent whites.

It however became apparent from the beginning that the legitimacy and capability of this endangered state to resolve the dispute within the communities(economic or ethnic), which have resulted in violence in the first place, will be used to measure whether this new government have been successful or not.

The nature of the South African economy is an important component of the democratization process. It is and will be an important factor in determining the success of the post- apartheid state. For example, South African business community have played crucial role in the peace process but the effectiveness of this process is handicapped by the socio-economic inequalities that permeates the society(a legacy of apartheid) and on which the business community have strived.

However pro-democracy they may be, an economy dominated by a white minority business and which reflect the self interest of the minority white cannot be expected to suddenly develop a moral obligation to protect the interest of all including the black majority, on whose back the economy was built lucratively and made productive during the apartheid era.

Violence remain therefore an intricate part of the south african political culture. It exalted an enormous toll on the black community for decades and the institution of universal suffrage cannot automatically dissipate its malignancy. The nature of the violence today differ only on its initiator. For decades and during the apartheid regime, violence was inflicted by the state, its military and its police but since 1990, its carried out within the black community as usual but only by blacks.

Mandela have responded to the violence by reorganizing the police department in an effort to turn it into a crime fighting agency rather than its usual role as a brutal enforcer of apartheid laws. But his effort is compounded by the lack of fund for training and lack of materials(such as vehicles) for enforcement.

There were other problems as well, the ANC have also been accused of abuse of power and cover-up. The removal of Winnie Mandela from of abuse of power and cover-up. The removal of Winnie Mandela from her post by President Mandela is an indication of the government trying to 'clean-house'. The ANC took steps to redress its credibility problem by setting up a disciplinary committee to investigate any violation of its constitution and codes of conduct(West Africa 4/6-12, 1995).Expectations are so high which if not met could undermine the efforts of this government. This is further compounded by high unemployment and white fear. Given the afore-mentioned, the task ahead is going to be difficult and the resulting schism should not be perceived as the end of the new South African State since there is always the tendency among observers of African politics to prematurely affirm the failures of these efforts.

The legacy of apartheid will continue to handicap the democratic efforts and it must be realized that democracy is new and it will take getting use to. Nelson Mandela is an important factor and a transitional leader but there are problems ahead especially on how his successor will chosen, accepted and respected will determine the consolidation of the efforts initiated during this transition period. The distribution of wealth and the guarantee of freedom is an important milestone in rekindling the sense of unity among South Africans. The mechanism of capital accumulation have changed and this will affect the level of surplus and investment in the new State and it is the responsibility of the leadership to increase the faith of the poor in the system and to sustain the belief of the rich in the political and economic program of the new government.

Notes:

African National Congress,(*1991)Strategic Documents(*On the ANC's Position on Power Sharing).
,(*1992)Report On the Deliberations of CODESA I & II*
,(*1993)Report on the Multiparty Conference(April 3, 1993.*
Fatton, R.,(1992),*Predatory Rule: The State and Society in Africa* (Boulder,CO: Lynne Rienner).
Greenberg, S (1980),*Race and State In Capitalist Development In South Africa : A Comparative Perspective*. (Johanesburg,SA: Raven Press).
Grundy, K.,(1986),*The Militarization of South African Politics.* (Bloomington: Indiana University Press).

Southern *Africa"Journal of Southern African Studies, 5,No.2.*

Laurence,P.(1994),"Mandela's First Hundred Days" *Africa Report,*November-December 1994.

Johnson, P. & Martin, D.*(1989)Apartheid Terrorism: The Destabilization Report*(London: James Currey).

Ohlson, T & Stedman, S.*(1994)The New is Not yet Born: Conflict Resolution in South Africa* (Washington DC: Brookings).

Ojo, B.(1992)" Nigerian and French Perspectives on the South African Question" in Jacob,H. & Omar, M.(ed). *France and Nigeria: Issues in Comparative Studies,* Ibadan: CREDU Documents).

Young, C.*(1994)The African Colonial State in Comparative Perspectives*(New Haven,CT: Yale University Press).

Zartman, W.*(1995)Collapse States: The Distingration and Restoration of Legitimate Authority*(Boulder,CO: Lynne Rienner Publ.).

Index

Abacha, Sanni, 59,128
Abiola, M.K.O, 39,56
African National Congress
(ANC), 155,157
Almond, Gabriel, 32
Apartheid, 158
Babangida, Ibrahim,
59,132,134
Bretton Woods, 34
Buganda, 91
Buhari/Idiagbon, 134
Buthelezi, M, 158
Census, 148
Clinton, William, 37
Conditionality, 33, 38
De Klerk, 157
Democracy, 26, 41
Diaby-Quattara, B, 70
Dunn, Kevin, 1,164
ECOMOG, 79
ECOWAS, 74
Gowon, Yakubu, 133
Huntington, Samuel, 44
Ibo, 42
Ihonvbere, Julius, 41, 64,164
IMF, 33,72
Lagos Plan of Action, 35
Mandela, Nelson, 157

Marxist, 42
Military, 52
Mitterrand, Francois, 38
Murtala, Mohammed, 59, 133,
140
Museveni, Yoweri, 42, 91, 96
Namibia, 114
Nigeria, 42, 57
Nuyoma, Sam, 124
Nyerere, Julius, 109
Obasanjo, Olusegun, 140, 143
146.
Obote, Milton, 92
O'hara, Thomas, 88,164
Ogunsuyi, Austin, 125,164
OAU, 35, 69
Ojo, Bamidele A.,
51,109,154,163
Party Politics, 147
Political development, 33
Praetorian tendency, 58
Resolution 435, 119
Rwanda, 29
Shagari,Shehu, 60, 133
Shonekan, Ernest, 138
Somide, Adegboyega, 24,165
South Africa, 156, 159
State, 55
State creation, 142
SWAPO, 120

Transition program, 139, 143
        148
Uganda, 42, 92
UN Program of Action for
African Economic Recovery &
Development, 36
UN Economic Commission for
Africa, 35, 40, 70

Walvis bay, 125
Yoruba, 43

ABOUT THE EDITOR

Bamidele A. Ojo

Associate Professor of Political science at Fairleigh Dickinson University. Bamidele received his Mphil and PhD from the University of Bordeaux. France and an LLM International Law from the University of Nottingham, England.He is also a graduate of the University of Ife ,Ife, Nigeria with a BSc. in Political Science and an MSc. in International Relations. He is the author of *Human Rights and the New World Order: Universality, Acceptability and Human Diversity* (New York: Nova Publishers, 1997), the editor of *The Nigeria's Third Republic: The Problems and Prospects of Transition to Civil Rule*(NY: Nova Publishers, 1998)and currently working on a monograph: SWAPO, NAMIBIA AND INTERNATIONAL POLITICS.And Bamidele has published extensively on African Politics (Nigeria, Namibia , South Africa, among others), International Relations and International Law. Dr Ojo is also the Executive-Director of the Council for Africanaffairs- a US based non profit research and educational foundation on African affairs

ABOUT CONTRIBUTORS:

Kevin DUNN.
An Visiting Professor at Tufts University Experimental College and at St Anselm College, Kevin taught at Boston College and Appalachian State University. Kevin also received his BA and MA from Davidson College, NC and Dalhousie University respectively and he is currently a doctoral candidate at Boston University.
He is currently working an *The Politics of Identity in Central Africa: Power, Representation and International Relations.*

Julius IHONVBERE:
Professor of Government at the University of Texas at Austin, Julius is currently a Program Officer at Ford Foundation. He has published extensively on Africa and Nigeria and received several awards for many of his outstanding and far reaching contribution to African studies.

Thomas J. O'HARA:
Associate Vice President for Academic Affairs ,Assistant Professor of Political Science and Holy Cross Hall Chaplain at King's College, Wilkes-Barre. PA, Thomas received his PhD from the American University in Washington DC and was a Professor of Political science at the Philosophical Centre of Jinga in Uganda. His recent publication includes papers on the Catholic lobby, the Politics of Abortion and the Rwanda crisis.

Austin O. OGUNSUYI:
An Assistant Professor of African Studies at Manhattanville College in New York, Austin received his PhD from Clark Atlanta University and a graduate of the Nigerian Institute of Journalism. Once a

Producer/Editor Cable News Network International CNNI in Atlanta ,GA. Dr Ogunsuyi has published and taught causes in comparative politics, African Diaspora and contemporary African politics.

Adegboyega SOMIDE:

Adegboyega is currently completing his doctorate at the Graduate School of Public Affairs, University of Albany- SUNY, where he is also teaches courses ranging from comparative politics to politics and government in Africa. Adegboyega's research interests includes the state and economic transformation in Africa. Ethnic groups and resource competition in Africa.